DIRK HESSEL
Awaken to Life

English translation
Ramey Rieger

Dirk Hessel

AWAKEN
TO
LIFE

A SPIRITUAL GUIDE TO YOUR TRUE SELF

Original title - Erkenntnis
© 2014 by Dirk Hessel

English translation by Ramey Rieger
doitwritetranslations@gmx.de

Awaken to Life
Copyright © 2020 by Dirk Hessel

Dirk Hessel
Mondsteinweg 29
D-33739 Bielefeld
Germany

The German National Library lists this publication in the German National
Bibliography; detailed bibliographic data can be found on the website at
http://dnb.dnb.de.

amazon edition
This book is also available in various eBook formats.

CONTENTS

Return to the Center

Probing and Insight

The Freedom of Being 227

Epilogue 255

Prologue

You may possibly view the title of this book with skepticism. You may think it promises you something unattainable in everyday, normal life.

And since we doubt that we can markedly improve our lives, or shy away from the necessary steps to do so, we scamper through our days; fearful of the future, railing against the past and brooding over problems, sometimes until the wee hours of the night.

Insight and a life of freedom would be lovely, but we'll stick to what we know – a life of worry with a smattering of joyful moments. At least there we know what to expect. No venturing into unknown waters.

And yet, sometimes, in a rare, quiet moment, we sense a loss. Something essential is missing. There is too little space given to our aspirations. It would be so nice to stop for a moment and reinvent ourselves or, at least, discover a new facet of our being. But we are driven. There is always this pressing need to accomplish something important, to keep the routine rolling.

Over the years, we have grown very intimate with our burden; we consider it normal. We push our deepest needs aside and are dissatisfied. And since we blame our surroundings instead of looking to ourselves, we beget friction and conflict.

We are convinced that our lives, restless and often over-loaded with appointments, are controlled by outside influences such as our job and relationships. That is not true. It is our thoughts and emotions that drive us and manipulate us.

One such driving force is the urgent feeling we must achieve something in life, an unsettling feeling that causes strife and fear, draining our vital energy. Yet we simply accept this vicious circle as a given, because what can we do when we can't pinpoint the cause? And even if we wanted to change the path we're on, where do we start? How can we redefine our reality?

At first glance, finding a substantial answer to these questions seems difficult. The path leading to a solution to our woes is blocked by an enormous misconception. Ever since we were children, we have believed we are an encapsulated I, destined to struggle through life; to strive and strain, and eventually, to die. Customarily, bringing this fallacy to light is no easy task, as it comprises our own, erroneous self-perception. We have a built-in distortion of reality, from which we look out at the world, expecting to find solutions. We believe we are seeing; we believe we know, but we are blind and misinformed.

This book is useful to clear your vision, helping you turn your sights inward. It is no happenstance that you are reading this book. You are obviously ready for pivotal awareness transformation.

Together, we will reveal the huge fraud behind the illusionary I, ultimately letting the soap bubble burst. The feeling of being disconnected; of being driven can dissolve. Our true being shines through. Finally, so many cares and woes fall away and we are free and truly at home.

How this book works

In the following chapters, we will clear away several inner barriers. These barriers most likely manifest themselves as external conflicts.

We set out by addressing the development of the human rational mind in childhood and teenage years, as this is where the fundamental attributes of the illusionary I – the ego – take shape. Our main interest, however, is in the present and all its challenges. Through self-exploration, the misconceptions our so-called rational mind produces are laid bare. To this end, you will occasionally encounter some simple attentive-ness exercises and mind games, recognizable by their *cursive headers*. Within this purposeful combination of text and exercises, you will recognize who you are *not*, so your errant self-image and all its related assumptions can fall away. Once these barriers have been cleared away, your true and joyous nature can emerge.

At this point, you should know that the ego is determined to hold tight to its adopted structures and the suffering they entail. The ego can only feel relatively secure in this environment. Therefore, certain sections of this book may arouse your suspicions because they do not jibe with your current perception of truth.

This subconscious resistance can trigger temporary weariness, impatience, boredom or testiness. Should this be the case with you, I recommend you perceive and accept this wave of resistance without judgment. It is your readiness to heed these words that opens your being for a new experience, laying the groundwork for profound joy in Life.

To be sure, there will still be turbulence, choppy seas and sometimes truly wild storms on the surface of your life. But these things pass, and on the ocean's floor, in the depth of your being, it is always peaceful and still.

Some statements in this book repeat themselves or change. This is intentional, and useful in navigating the dense jungle of thoughts and emotions to reach your destination, inner peace.

The following words were not bred by a rational mind and are not intended for a rational mind. They come directly from a source and are directed toward a source – the truth of who you are. You could say, Life wrote this book and is reading this book to awaken from the illusionary I.

Please read all chapters in their intended, consecutive order, allowing their full impact to enfold and new insights to take effect. Take your time, find your own pace and allow new insights to penetrate your being. Sometimes, it is fitting to let the book sink; to stop reading and simply sit in silence. You will know when.

The point is to follow your impulses, to open your heart to the written word, to allow for the necessary pauses for integrating what you have read. Gradually, you will feel lighter, more in balance and alive. Then, you won't need a book or exercises anymore.

And now, step into the free Life that you are.

Thought Clouds

A few days ago, while walking through the park on a beautiful, sunny day, I had an interesting encounter. A woman walking by stopped and looked at me for second before commenting sourly, »It's awfully warm today.« I replied, »Yes, it's a beautiful day, isn't it?« The woman countered thoughtfully, »Perhaps. But it's supposed to get cold again soon.« She frowned darkly and walked away.

Had she heard the weather forecast and the prospect of colder weather had triggered thoughts responsible for her bad mood? If so, then she had several clouds in her head. She had the image of heavy clouds that were possibly looming on the horizon as well as the even darker clouds of her own thoughts. All that on such a perfectly beautiful, sunny day.

It may be hard to believe, but this is how most people spend their lives. Imprisoned in worries about the future or resentment against the past. Or both at once. Constantly nagging, deceiving thought patterns prevent nearly every person on this Earth from giving their undivided attention to the only meaningful thing in life – the present moment.

When awareness is obscured by a mental veil, Life's beauty and joys cannot penetrate the barrier. We feel isolated and our sense of security is dependent on how much we have under control. How did this happen?

Our inner world is populated with our thoughts and emotions, all of which have an attribute we rarely perceive. They are *magnetic*.

In relationship to our five senses, seeing, hearing, feeling, smelling and touching, thinking could simply be another sense, sharing an equal percentage of our attention. But thoughts contain an abundance of the words *I, me, my,* and *mine*, and this personal reference crowds out other input.

Thoughts and emotions draw the greater part of our attention like a powerful magnet, monopolizing our energies. Hypnotized by our inner theatrics, we are spellbound, listening to them and taking them for truth. We are trapped in a myopic existence.

The result is an extremely limited self-perception. And since excessive and predominantly negative thinking is an enormous strain on our bodies and minds, we are susceptible to illness and disease. Focusing on our thoughts, we walk around wearing blinders, sequestered from Life's abundance, living in an oppressive, self-absorbed cosmos.

Take a look around you. Observe the distant expression in many peoples' eyes, their grim faces, their harassed demeanor or their empty preoccupation with their cellphones, some even engaged in loud monologues.

This condition is very far removed from the opulence Life offers. A perpetual deluge of thoughts has taken control, herding us through life at top speed without a moment's pause for the present.

Does this sound familiar? And you ask yourself, »What can I do? How can I attain more serenity, more awareness of the present moment, free from my permanently disruptive inner monologue?«

The answer lies within your true self. For a calm and clear perception, it is enough to simply recognize and accept your inner bustle. The moment you identify your thoughts, allowing them to exist without judgment or participation, i.e. commenting on the perpetual commentary, they begin to change or dissolve. The overwhelming burden of hypnotic, inundating thought is lifted as you recognize it for what it is, a baseless and meaningless phenomenon emerging within you.

When you no longer identify with your mental world, you are free, living in healthy balance between times of thought and times of stillness. Tranquility brings you much closer to the source of your true nature. You become more attentive; you perceive your living oneness with Life and are liberated from the tyranny of your rational mind.

The Apple

Here, you will discover both how excessive thinking and the emotions it triggers influence our lives, and how you can break free of this debilitating condition.

Much of what goes on inside of us takes place beneath the surface of our consciousness; we are quite unaware of what's going on. Thus, there are many situations in life where we are convinced that there is nothing we can do to change things.

The bulk of our inner images, thoughts and feelings create the person we believe we are, so we rarely question our reality. Yet, when we learn to distance ourselves from this habituated process, it becomes clear that, for years, our lives have been controlled by chimeras that have absolutely nothing to do with our true being.

With this first mind game, you set out to discover your free nature. I am going to give you a sentence and ask you to think it silently in your mind three times, with your eyes closed. It makes no difference if while you are thinking the sentence, letters appear, or images or emotions, or all of them at once. After you have thought the sentence, open your eyes and continue reading.

Now close your eyes and think three times,
»The apple is hanging on the tree.«

Did you think, »The apple is hanging on the tree« three times? How do you know you thought the sentence three times?

Reflect a moment on what your answer could be
and then continue reading.

Which answer did you find? Did you count how many times you thought the sentence? Or did you hear the sentence in your mind? Or maybe you saw a picture of an apple tree in your mind's eye. All these answers may be true, but you probably did not hit upon the most important insight into this mind game.

This leads to two additional questions. Was the sentence, as it emerged in your mind, acknowledged in any way? (How is not important.) And is there something like an *inner, silent witness* inside you, that observes you as you think the apple sentence?

If the answer is yes, and you noticed the silent observer, you have made an essential discovery. If the answer is no, simply read on, or repeat the mind game, if you like.

Recognizing the perceiver, who can observe thoughts and images as they arise, also means that you are not your thoughts. You are simply the one who registers the incoming content. The perceiver is much more than content. Therefore, it makes no difference what the thoughts and images portray, or how important they seem.

When the thought arises, »I have to go shopping«, it has as little to do with your true self as the apple sentence has.

During childhood, our system governing thought and emotion was shaped in such way, that we have had complete faith in it ever since. Usually, we are born in the country where our mother tongue is spoken. As small children, we soon parrot a few words, making new sentences. A world emerges wherein thousands of thoughts arise and dissolve, like countless inscribed balloons rising into the sky, only to float away on the wind. We attach enormous importance to these letters. We are convinced they all have something to do with us personally, thus requiring our undivided attention.

We mistakenly set our inner life on the same level as our true self. We assume all statements, particularly those with I-related words, are the naked truth. But an *I must…* in your rational mind does *not* mean you *must* do anything. Those are only a bunch of letters of the alphabet, shaping seemingly important words. Where do these words come from? We will look at that in detail in a later chapter.

Taking the example of *I must go shopping*, the main point is that you don't *have to* go shopping. You *can* go shopping or you can skip the shopping, regardless of what the thought says.

You are not the person your thoughts are addressing, you are a being observing the thoughts. What you now need is a fundamental change in perspective. Let the compass of your attention, that has, until now, been pointing toward the outside world and your thoughts and feelings, make a 180° turn. Allow your attention to penetrate your inner world, zooming in on your Self, the silent observer in the background. In reality, this is who you are. And this is what you are here to discover. The silent witness, the perception or the space in which all content appears.

To give you a taste of what is to come, we could say that you are both the space *and* the content. This is the true Self you seek. The Facilitator of longed-for serenity and stability. The Being that has, up to now, been overlooked by focusing on the endless deluge of thoughts.

The Pendulum

During one normal day, thousands upon thousands of thoughts occur in our rational mind. That a greater portion of our life's energies is wasted on excessive thinking is more than exhausting. Self-observation also reveals that many of your thoughts are negative and/or repetitive; that you often find yourself brooding over one single issue.

As you know from experience, thinking about an approaching event can just as well trigger dread as it can joyful anticipation. As a result, these years of repetitive, negative thought patterns can have a corrosive impact on our bodies and minds.

Assume you are extremely furious at someone and say, »The mere thought of him/her makes me sick to my stomach!« And it's true, just thinking about the person ties a knot in your stomach. But, contrary to what you may have thus far believed, you do not get a stomachache because you are truly furious and your body agrees by clenching its stomach. The thought, »I hate him«, is nothing more than a distorted, ego imagining, reinforced by the body's emotional reaction and physical contraction.

Imagine a human being in balance, healthy in body and soul, as a pendulum at rest. When the organism is constantly bombarded with negative thoughts such as, »I'm furious«, »That's wrong«, »I'm not good enough«, or »I really must get this right«, a person's health eventually falls out of kilter. The pendulum swings higher, intensifying illnesses.

Many illnesses of body and soul have taken this path, created by debilitating thought patterns. When the disruptive patterns are identified and dethroned, it may take quite a while for the body to follow the mind and come into balance. Yet it is possible.

You may ask yourself why we are subjected to such challenges; what's the point of such a life? External circumstances carry no foul intent, they simply hold up a mirror, reflecting our inner world, urging us to make healthy changes, leading to a deeper awareness. Discovering who you are and who you are not, reveals the origin of your worries and alleged problems.

When erroneous thoughts vanish, you are able to lead a free life. Naturally, there will still be challenging situations, negative thought processes and unwelcome emotions. But you will recognize them for what they are, an appeal for you to become more aware. In the course of time, you will be less prone to emotional and imagined entanglements. You will take things less personally, and, most importantly, less seriously. You will be happy, recognizing yourself as Life itself.

Stop thinking

Are you convinced that you need only keep your rational living room clean and body and soul will be immune to imbalance? *Keeping your thoughts under control will have a positive impact on your words, deeds and being.*

This advice can be found in many different books, and it seems logical. You've probably also heard the adage, *Thoughts are free.* But can you really think what you want to think? The next experiment will give you excellent idea about just how free your thoughts are.

Immediately stop all thoughts for thirty seconds.

Did it work? Probably not. You cannot deliberately decide what to think, as your thoughts continue to arise without your permission. The rational mind, with its deluge of thought cannot be stopped by *you.* This is because we are not the independent thinkers, we are the thought. Life is the creator of this thought, manifesting itself in a myriad of varieties. Why it thinks like this in one body, and like that in another, remains a mystery.

An *I* cannot influence thoughts, as it is a thought itself. Yet experiences in many spiritual traditions have shown that by simply recognizing the thought deluge, it recedes, making space for a life of more well-being and ease.

Introspection

Observe yourself at this very moment. See how you are holding this book in our hands; how you are reading the words.

Do you really think that *you* are turning the pages; *you* that occasionally blink or scratch an itch? Can a conceptual *I* tilt his/her head when he/she questions a sentence just read? Or can this *I* control the complex bodily processes such as muscle response, metabolism and blood circulation? Is thought necessary to turn a page?

Try it out, right now. If turning pages is not accompanied by a conceptual commentary, then who is turning the pages?

Perhaps you think you carry out many of these actions unconsciously and automatically; that they do not require any thought. And it's true, all bodily actions are created and navigated. Just not by an individual *you*, but by the Life that you are. This is the essential difference. And where freedom lies.

Realizing this is essentially very easy, since nothing else exists. But our view of it has been veiled by conceptual assumptions that have been piling up inside us since we entered this life. We carry within us an enormous mountain of imaginings about what we perceive outside of us and what we believe ourselves to be. The misconception that these imaginings compose our true identity, leads to a feeling of imprisonment, instead of one of freedom and satisfaction.

We take our unverified assumptions seriously; believe they are who we are, putting ourselves completely and utterly at the mercy of an uncontrollable inner force. New, imagined misconceptions perpetually arise and vanish, making it impossible to discover our genuine, enduring anchor.

Our momentary self-image is built on precarious, vulnerable and, most importantly, highly transient thought forms. How can we possibly establish a foundation of profound peace and security?

It is as if we are careening through whitewater, clinging to a tiny piece of driftwood, calling the driftwood *me*. It's no wonder that we are constantly going under, bobbing up, wrenched this way and that way.

Luckily, you are not what you think. The solid foundation, your enduring anchor, is already within you. You are the river, flowing quietly and steadily beneath the turbulent surface.

The Rational Mind and Ego

This would be a good point to define the terms *rational mind* and *ego*, as it is the mechanism behind these two words that so powerfully influences our lives. Although rational mind and ego are two different terms, they both indicate the same inner entity.

The rational mind is commonly understood to be a sovereign thought-machine governed by intelligent, systematic methods. It is allegedly a biological super-computer, absorbing input and generating output. We rarely question this mechanism because it seems to serve us well in our everyday lives.

But our entire inner life shows a very different picture - a being cowed and threatened by years of conditioning. For this reason, I define the term *ego* as our reactive sense of self that fears attacks from the environment.

The combination of misconceptions, the so-called rational mind, and the corresponding emotions, creates the fallacy that each and every one of us is an isolated, singular entity. We have been conditioned since our earliest childhood to identify with our thoughts and emotions and put unquestioning faith in our inner bustle. We are thoroughly convinced that it is *I* that acts and feels a particular way; *I* who reacts to individual situations.

The spurious being *ego* defines itself over a variety of mechanisms. It must compare itself with others to create a position in which it feels secure. From the ego's point of view, the optimal position is higher, better, nobler or more spiritual than its rival. To attain this position, the current rival is watched with eagle eyes, his or her actions are evaluated and the resulting judgment is filed away in a waiting drawer.

The ego then applies the appropriate words or actions to place itself in the right light, where it believes to have a possible position of power or control. Of course, there remains a latent fear of being unseated, but it is momentarily less tangible.

As a rule, we react automatically to a given situation, drawing from the database of our mental conditioning. We rarely consciously observe a situation and act accordingly. If our pool of mental mechanisms falls short of what is necessary to triumph, i.e. to maintain our position in a given conflict, our ego is clever enough to generate new tactics.

By identifying with our thought and emotions, any confrontation feels like an attack on our Self. And the rational mind responds by pulling all stops. It battles, fights, surrenders and/or flatters – anything to safeguard our existent thought patterns from damage. We subconsciously believe they are an essential part of our Self, our so-called identity; and must be protected at all costs in order for us to survive.

Just watching the news or talk shows on TV makes it obviously clear how thought patterns control humans. Whether addressing a military conflict, an act of terror, an economic battle, or a common, everyday political discussion it is nearly always about the ego striving to out-maneuver its opponent. I am what I think! Therefore, my thoughts must be defended to the last, even if a verbal or physical attack is necessary.

This exhausting, misleading existence has been controlling and abusing humanity for thousands of years, resulting in endless conflicts, oppression, wars, and destruction. To put an end to this vicious circle, we must strive for a dramatic change in consciousness.

This doesn't mean, though, that our rational mind is an enemy we must banish. That's neither necessary nor possible – the rational mind is an equally valid part of Life.

This book focuses on re-establishing a healthy balance between mental activity and inner tranquility. When our awareness is not entangled in the illusion of an independent I, the rational mind is an outstanding tool for tending to practical affairs. Attempting to reject our rational mind, or our ego for that matter, doesn't help us in the least. What helps is to get a clear view of mental activities and not take them so seriously.

Recognizing what lies beyond the rational mind – your true Self – brings balance back to body and soul. Understand that you are first and foremost a silent witness, a perceiving aware-ness, and not the deluge of thoughts and emotions flowing through you. When these two are relegated to their proper dimension, energy and love of life are renewed. You no longer identify with an illusionary I. Your awakened being and conscious actions have a positive impact on your surroundings – and on humanity as a whole.

Childhood and Youth

You have always had an inkling that your true Self encompasses more than what you have thus far perceived. This book aims to turn that inkling into an experience.

To fulfill that aim, we will need to go back into the past for a moment and look at the myriad of thought and emotional patterns we developed back then, and which still influence us today. We cannot simply ignore our inner commotion. It is absurd to simply hope that, without any effort on your part, Life will unfold in full bloom, and you can serenely set sail for awareness.

The moment rough and rocky seas – worries and problems – disrupt the surface of your existence, you will eventually be swept away on your disappointment in life.

Taking the time now to look at your inner life, instead of trying to circumvent it, you will gradually find stillness and the light you are can shine out in all its brilliance.

What never changed?

Look back, and remember a scene from your childhood. You were four or five years old. Maybe in your room, or outside in the garden, you were completely absorbed in play, at one with yourself and the universe. Occasionally, you looked up and inspected your surroundings.

Years later, as a teenager, you revised your concept of who you are. Yet perhaps you can remember a situation from this time, too, where you felt a oneness with yourself and everything around you.

Now, you are an adult. You define yourself as an autonomous being with an adult identity. You feel quite differently than you did at other ages you have traversed on the path to maturity. Still, you experience moments of unity.

Throughout your life, your identity has continuously changed, yet there is one feeling, one state of being that has never changed. Do you know what I'm talking about? Take a moment to reflect. Got it? Now, read on.

Yes, I'm talking about the awareness of your own presence. That profound knowledge, *I am*, regardless of how you define yourself or of what you are doing at the moment. In the background of our everyday lives lies a generally unacknowledged consciousness of our existence. You could define this with the words, *I live*.

Only when you learn to think less, can you fully perceive your living consciousness. But it is already there, the inner, conscious light of your true nature, shining through at special moments. It is a gift. It is precious. It keeps us alive.

Turn your senses inward.
Can you feel how alive you are?

The seed of separation

A new-born child is unaware of the looming sense of separation that is the genesis of a future beset with problems. The infant does not yet know the difference between here and there, inner and outer, self and other. The tiny being has yet to realize it has already left the secure unity from whence it came. Snug at the mother's breast, the baby feels as secure as before birth.

But the first time the baby is left alone, she immediately senses the loss. Uncertain and afraid, the baby cries to call her mother back to restore the sense of unity and security.

You will certainly not remember the first time this happened. Perhaps your parents looked down at you and called you by name, which meant nothing to you as an infant. You had no mental concept of you and I, me and others. This was a language you could not speak.

Eventually, though, you came to realize, »I am the one they are pointing at; I am the name they are calling. That is me.« The eternal oneness you came from and still felt within you suddenly shrank to a tiny being of flesh and blood. Where I was once at one with all creation and felt secure in vastness, I now find myself limited to this small body. The emerging perception of boundaries between me and others, of separation, transforms a familiar eternity into something overwhelmingly huge, uncontrollable and threatening.

I have become vulnerable.

This is the most pivotal experience in human existence. It invokes terror – the terror of separation. The young human being is severed from the loving oneness of Life and catapulted into an unknown, threatening world.

Our immediate response is to gradually install a security system to protect us from this fearful and ominous world. Any unknown factor must find a place within the system, it must become recognizable to me and thus, controllable.

This is the birth of the rational mind and learning. The eternal oneness I was born into is dissected into individual terms and mental concepts. Every manifestation, every object receives a label, a name.

A complex system of fraudulent security is contrived, leading me to believe that I can recognize, allocate and assess all things. I no longer live in terror of the world. Depending on the given situation, I need only call up, apply and, if necessary, defend myself with the corresponding mental concept.

Yet, quickly, inevitably, despite all my efforts, I discover that my control and security system is precarious and easily penetrated. I am still susceptible to fear; the world is still ominous and I can still be swallowed up by its enormity. As I mature, my fear also grows in width and depth. The mechanism of the rational mind cultivates an entity with independent attributes; an entity that must assert itself in a world apparently rife with adversity – the ego.

Most likely, you had many beautiful childhood experiences. Your parents raised you and cared for you as best as they could, according to their level of awareness. Nature's design dictates that a child's survival is dependent on their parents', or persons acting as such, protection.

Despite the beauty of this design, the greater part of negative thought patterns is developed in childhood. In the Theater of Life, we encounter challenges to surmount very early on. It is quite possible we will never understand why certain things happen to us. Nevertheless, all these challenges, no matter how difficult, are stepping stones to expanding our consciousness. This includes the years we are dependent on our parents. Although these formative years are often painful, they are an elementary phase of Life.

Whatever happened, was supposed to happen. Nothing could have been otherwise.

And now, your adult life is burdened with subconscious thought patterns and reflexes which were activated, and have continued to be active, since your childhood. The good news is that you now have the ability to expose and release them. This is not an option for a child.

Something's wrong with me

Do you remember the time when you were very small and wished for the moon?

Open-hearted, you joyfully announced your wishes to your parents. For some reason, your parents could not respond appropriately and denied you your wish. Maybe they were distracted and couldn't give your request the attention you hoped for. Maybe they misunderstood you.

Usually, your parents did their best to give you what you needed or at least comforted you when things turned out differently than you wished. You may have occasionally even understood why they denied you something, and accepted their decision. All the same, you felt personally rejected, were angry or sad without knowing why.

Most of our parents were also denied the authentic and spontaneous expression of their innermost desires. Just like you, suppressing their naturalness caused them soul-felt anguish. Nobody wants to feel pain, so they relegated theirs to a far corner of their soul.

Your needs remind your parents of their own loss, that they could not express themselves the way they naturally would have done. Thus, when you express a deep desire, their repressed pain immediately surfaces, and is usually expressed with annoyance or grief. But they naturally don't want to feel this pain, so it must be denied. Thus, your parents' subconscious defense mechanism must also deny you your deepest desires. Maybe you had to satisfy yourself with such standard phrases like, »not now«, »be quiet« or »give it a rest.«

As a result, your tender Self began to believe, »there's something wrong with me. I am not good enough.« This tragic misconception is responsible for a whole slew of future behavioral entanglements and vicious circles as it spawns the conviction, »I must be different to be worthy of love.«

The moment this delusion takes root and grows, your life becomes straining and complicated. Your innate ability to meet Life's challenges consciously and without ceremony is drastically diminished. Instead, you place your faith in fallacies.

Your parents would have been shocked, had they registered what was going on inside of you. They did not intentionally do you harm. They loved you and did their best to help you grow into an independent being. And still you felt you had to change; felt something was wrong with you.

This distorted perspective has influenced you since your childhood, exactly as it had influenced your parents since their childhood. You are convinced that most of your dreams will not come true.

»If I follow my heart's desire, I will never arrive there. Stones will be thrown in my path, I will be ignored or, even worse, punished.« Most likely you still think and feel this way. You yourself are the greatest stone on the path to your heart's desire. You are blocked by subconscious defense mechanisms, spontaneous illnesses or accidents.

And, doubtlessly, your ever-active rational mind has seemingly irrefutable arguments, to keep you – for heaven's sake! – from fulfilling your deepest dreams.

I want to be someone else

Even with a good roof over their heads, many children do not feel at home. Their parents might have financial worries, may be unhappy or their jobs leave them little time.

Maybe the child is one of many and there is no space for individual nurturing. The child feels neglected and a growing rage against his or her parents causes a deep, damaging rift between them. The child's negative motto is, »no one sees me.«

But the child is trapped. Wholly dependent on his parents or guardians for survival, he must secure their support at all costs, even though he feels unloved and unacknowledged.

Convinced he is not worthy of love and recognition, the young human being comes to a tragic conclusion, »I must change who I am if I want to be loved and noticed.«

Without a clue, as to how to do this, the child begins to experiment with a variety of behaviors, searching for one that seems to work. Willing to go to any extreme, he would much rather receive negative attention, punishments and such, rather than be completely ignored. At least he's noticed, that's the main thing. Once the child has found a behavior pattern that has the desired effect, he hones and refines it, to maintain his contact with his parents and surroundings.

If, however, all attempts to earn recognition fail, the child will eventually give up, withdrawing herself completely. This inner isolation can lead to severe psychological and physical disorders.

From the child-ego's perspective, various methods for surviving the parental home seem to work. Yet at this tender age, she cannot steer her behavior in a wholesome direction without guidance. Her ego's survival strategies take root and continue to grow, without her or her parents having the faintest idea.

Imagine you are a child sitting in your room, playing contentedly with your toys. Suddenly, you hear your parents shouting in the next room. Unsettled, you go to see what the trouble is. As soon as you see your parents, you know something's wrong, but they tell you just the opposite. They insist everything's just fine, there's no need to worry.

You are then plagued with conflicting emotions. Your parents say everything's fine and your instinct tells you something is wrong. Since you are absolutely dependent on your parent 'gods,' on their opinions and decisions, you have no choice but to believe them. Thus, a tragedy takes place. If your parents are always right, then logically, your perceptions must be wrong.

Should this situation often occur, you begin to assume your feelings and perceptions are unreliable, are suspiciously errant. You stop believing your own senses and lose your most precious possession – your self-trust.

Something quintessential has changed in your tender life. You no longer heed your inner, natural-born voice that could safely guide you through Life. You now rely on the dictates of your surroundings, accommodating expectations that are not necessarily in agreement with your needs. This dependence on external opinions grows stronger as you grow older, triggering a plethora of situations where your core feeling is helplessness.

You become more and more adept at quickly absorbing others' opinions, making them your own, leaving no opportunity to expose them as fallacies. Quite the contrary, you believe these thoughts are who you are and begin to defend and protect them.

From the firm belief, »something's wrong with me«, grows the credo »I want to be someone else.« Children quickly learn that they cannot fulfill all their wishes and that they most likely have no right to fulfillment.

Home life is full of schedules and rules, and a child eventually regards what his parents say and do as truer and weightier than his own perceptions. When his behavior is primarily aligned with his parents' opinions, he is exposed to fewer conflicts. By adapting himself, his parents' love and attention are much more accessible. And that is the fundamental goal of any child.

Sometimes a child goes so far as to regard every viewpoint and value judgment her parents hold as true. To avoid making waves or becoming a black sheep, which would put her in a traitorous spotlight, the thought occurs, »I mustn't go any further than my parents have.«

This subconscious mental attitude is yet another hurdle in a human's free developmental path. Without a conscious clue as to why, the child chooses a similar, or the same, profession as her parents and is careful not to achieve a greater level of success.

A subconscious and deep-seated fear of rejection and withdrawal of affections can clip the adult child's wings so short, she cannot fly beyond the next street or two. Or she moves on to create a family constellation exactly as the one from whence she came. Perhaps his parents have led the child to believe he could choose a better profession than the one the parents chose, or they expressed a wish for grandchildren. A timid child will do his best to fulfill these desires, to avoid conflict at all costs.

Although this conforming behavior is the picture of harmony, resentment against and grief over not having followed his true desires simmer beneath the surface.

Throughout the course of development, a child is repeatedly haunted by her inner voice. Never entirely silent, and more accessible to children than to adults, the inner voice of her true nature calls out to her. Thus, a conflict arises between her true nature, bidding her to listen to her natural perceptions, and the growing force of her ego.

This rift causes intense strain and the child subconsciously connects the pressure to her parents and their demands. At the same time, she is dependent on her parents' love and recognition.

The child vacillates between her longing for love and her rage against and rejection of authority. Parents are rarely aware of their child's inner conflict. To the best of their ability, they strive to meet their child's needs and prepare her – from their point of view – for a successful life. The child, however, feels hopelessly trapped.

A desperate decision

In the meantime, the growing child has become accustomed to functioning within the family structure. Yet, the older he becomes and the less dependent he is on his parents, the louder his own desires call out for fulfillment.

His parents obviously cannot answer the call and they often fail to give the teenager the support and sheltering in a way that he can both recognize and accept. This cements his conviction that his true desires are invisible to his parents. He has learned to act accordingly for short-term advantages, but has the feeling that everyone is only interested in themselves.

This discomforting scenario is compounded by his parents' frequent lack of time and sympathy. Below the threshold, ferments an urgent feeling of »I've got to get out of here soon somehow.« The dilemma is *how*, since he is still dependent on his parents.

The daily family routine leaves the youth bewildered and discontent. Her sense of isolation leads her to make a desperate decision. »I don't know where on this Earth I can feel secure. I don't really trust anyone and I'm furious. I hardly ever get what I truly wish I had – authentic attention. I've had enough. From now on, I'll take care of myself, by myself.«

And from this moment on, a young person chooses a life of isolation, no matter how her relationships appear on the outside. By the power of her young ego she has withdrawn as far as possible from her naturalness, burying her joyful being and is no longer linked to Life.

Survival strategies

The ego's will to survive urges us to develop a number of strategies very early on, to maintain control over apparently threatening situations at home and around us. For example, a child may develop a high intelligence and quick tongue to deflect harmful situations.

The ego believes, »When I can assess a situation quickly, weigh the options, process and file the information, then I will be safe; I will survive.« At first glance, this may appear to be a desirable trait, and as a matter of fact, intelligence is the Holy Grail of our day.

Many parents want their children to be high achievers, believing they will then have a better chance of success. They do not see the burden they place on their children's shoulders. You have probably often heard the maxim *knowledge is power*, and may even believe it to be true. But we rarely realize that knowledge is only thought in an ordered sequence, a straight-jacket of presumptuousness.

As a firewall for the ego, intelligence is an excellent, multi-functional tool. Our precarious thought structure wants to be better than any other, to ensure more self-security. On the flip side of the intellectual coin, while perpetually on the lookout for competitors – »no one can be cleverer, better educated or more successful than I am« – we forfeit sponta-neity and levity. Constantly wary of possible contenders for the status of smartest, our lives become exhaustingly rigid. But the status must be held at all costs.

Since our ego defines itself by its outstanding acuity, a sense of inferiority is unbearable. The actual number of thought patterns also plays a vital role. If *my* thoughts dominate a discussion or argument, then I am more important, bigger and more valuable than my counterpart. This sense of triumph confirms the ego's illusion of stability, it feels less vulnerable for a while. »The more and faster I think, the better I am.«

A child's ego develops other survival strategies to avert conflicts and rejection. Exaggerated diplomacy and flattery are two such strategies. Often, a healthy sense of self defense or inner justice is compromised in challenging situations. It is pushed aside with the argument, »If I want to please my parents, teachers, friends, I'll keep my thoughts to myself.« This striving to be everything for everyone is carried on into adult life, at work, in relationships and in family life.

Another child subconsciously chooses withdrawal to protect himself from unsettling situations and from rejection. The result can be learning difficulties, passivity and other psychological disorders. By choosing non-functionality, apparent threats from the outside world are kept at bay. The creed here is »Leave me alone.«

And then there is the warrior, confronting whatever Life presents to her with fury and rebellion. In this case, the ego shields its vulnerability with an offensive strategy, posing as strength and aggression.

All these activities emerging from the rational mind are subconscious. Not one of them is an intentional act of free will. The ego strategies described here do not apply to every person. But as you have probably recognized in yourself, they apply to many.

It cannot be said often enough; your parents cannot be given the blame for what occurred in your childhood and youth. They acted to the best of their ability according to their level of consciousness. Only the wise can act wisely.

Above, you have read several examples of how a child's ego can manifest itself, generating a stressful, unhappy future life. Maybe you have recognized yourself in one or more of the examples, all of which may occur in varying degrees or combinations.

The beauty of it is, when you recognize and accept these corrupting mechanisms, you go a goodly way toward positive change in your everyday life, bringing about greater awareness of yourself and of your surroundings.

Help your children

If you should have children in your care, establish authentic contact with them. Perhaps, you can take your child in your arms and say to him, »You are fine the way you are. You can be however you like and that is the way I love you. There's nothing you have to do for me and I'm happy you are here.«

These words and deeds are balsam to a child's soul, knowing she mustn't bend herself to your needs. She learns to trust and gains self-assurance. But of course, you must walk what you talk and not bend to anyone else's needs, either. A caring attitude toward yourself is the first prerequisite for caring and accepting other human beings. When you express yourself authentically, you create an authentic environment for your children, and those around follow your example. We will talk at length about how this works later.

Maybe your childhood was completely different and you had the freedom to express and develop your desires. In this case, you are not particularly burdened with the above described thought patterns. But it is more likely that you recognized yourself in at least one of the scenarios.

On your path to a fulfilling existence, you will need to integrate these insights, as well as other revelations whose impact extends much further than a happy or unhappy childhood. Let's move on now to the present tense, to the world of adulthood.

All Grown Up

Convictions and conclusions embedded throughout childhood and youth take root and grow with us, powerfully influencing our adult life. They often drive us to do things that are in direct conflict with our deepest desires for self-fulfillment.

The following pages offer descriptions of behavior patterns. Not all of them may apply to you, but it's quite possible that some of them, in some form, ring a bell. In this case, by simply recognizing and accepting behavior patterns, the means to discard them is placed in your hand.

Role games

Do you volunteer to work extra hours at your job, drawing your superior's attention and praise? Do you offer your help to friends, denying yourself the leisure time you need to refill your energy reserves? Do accept invitations to social get-togethers although you would rather not go?

You do these things hoping to reap the rewards of love and recognition. Fear of rejection, of withdrawal of affection and of isolation drives you to be and act differently than you really are, without granting you the desired feeling of genuine connection. This behavior is brought about by the thought pattern »I want to be someone else.« It keeps you from finding what you are looking for – equanimity, warm encounters and inner freedom. Your peace of mind and health are damaged by an old thought pattern. Your complete faith in what you think veils the fallacy, and you following the dictates of your illusory I.

Situations, problems or statements that rattle the cage of your conditioning are met with justification, testiness, sadness or anger. Although you are confronted with a situation you cannot cope with alone, you are too proud or too suspicious to accept help. Offers of help from caring friends seeking to share the burden or point you in a new direction are accepted reluctantly or not at all. If you take their advice to heart, you will have to leave your well-trodden path.

There could be a whole slew of life situations where you feel powerless and incensed, but you hold to your conviction that help is only for weaklings. Everything you aim to do must be done alone, without anyone else's meddling. And although you insist on your independence, there is a growing, obscure yearning for genuine affection and appreciation. You are trapped in an encrypted vicious circle.

Maybe you have been in a relationship for quite some time, yet you are incapable of an authentic, profound rapport because you don't completely trust anyone. If someone were to offer their heart unconditionally, on a silver platter, you would immediately start looking for the hidden catch. You view your surroundings at a critical distance, and hardly anyone is good enough to fulfill your demands.

You are sitting in a snare of your own making, which took effect long ago when you drew up the contract stating, »From now on, I'll take care of myself, by myself.« You have long forgotten the conditions of the deal, or why you made it in the first place, but all stipulations are still in effect.

In moments of deep intimacy, you are often unable to surrender completely. A pronounced escape reflex requires you to withdraw from a relationship and hold fast to your independence. The strain arising between your longing for authentic intimacy and your childhood fear of rejection nags at you. You inject unhealthy anesthetics against the pain - shopping, eating, watching television, excessive sex, alcohol or drugs.

But the sense of loss merely intensifies and you feel hopelessly at the mercy of life's caprices. To avert complete collapse, a wounded ego's defensive reaction may be to harden itself against the pain. To protect your ego, you become cynical or sarcastic, spewing stinging, yet apparently accurate, judgments on your nearest and dearest. You become sharp-sighted in detecting the absurdities of life, often accompanied with a sharp tongue, as well. These attributes bring you attention and superficial admiration.

Your quick wit and high spirits are infectious, an excellent remedy for invisibility and isolation. The role of a clever, independent and amusing life-of-the-party is tailor-made for you and offers the ideal camouflage for your true soul condition.

Yet eventually, sadness and inner isolation overpower the need to play the witty, entertaining clown. A small voice tells you that your behavior does not in the least reflect who you truly are, and that is it time for a personal change.

You have played your role before your family, friends and acquaintances with the utmost conviction, but it's enough now, you are too exhausted to keep up the façade. While considering your options for change, the outside world hasn't a clue as to what's going on inside of you and continues to call for the entertainer, expecting you to stay true to the role.

In the end, unable to present a viable alternative, you succumb to external pressure, to the increasingly loud discomfort of your inner voice.

Maybe you have convinced yourself that there are other people much worse off than you are. Maybe you believe that your tug-of-war dilemma is simply a part of life.

There are, of course, other roles played in life. One of these is the merciful nurse.

You strive to help everyone no matter what the situation, but you rarely receive help yourself. You occasionally gripe over a lack of support, but on the whole, you feel at home in the self-sacrificing role. Since all your energies are directed outward toward helping others, you have little time to acknowledge and satisfy your own true desires.

In fact, you are very rarely aware that you even have any. Thus, you do not feel the need to confront your yearning for true, unconditional love or to feel the pain of loss non-fulfillment awakens. Then again, by not allowing anyone to get close to you, you reap other advantages. This one-sided relationship you maintain with your environment reduces the risk of disappointment or hurt enormously.

And yet, fear also keeps out the most important relationship in your life – the relationship with your true self, unconditional love that you are.

There are so many roles we believe we have to play.
Which role is yours?

Cancel the agreement

When you want to disentangle yourself from your self-made snare, you must cancel the agreement you made with yourself in your childhood – »I will take care of myself, by myself.«

When you have had enough of playing the clown, the cynic, the merciful nurse or any other role, go to a place where you feel safe. Sit down and say to yourself, »As of right now, I choose to come out of my isolation. I no longer want to be lonely. I want to be connected. I want to be kind, to myself and to the world. I can allow myself genuine intimacy. I feel good without my mask. True relationships neither kill nor hurt me, they strengthen and fulfill me.«

Of course, you can find and use your own words for this declaration. Decisive is that you cancel the old agreement from the depths of your heart, directing your rage and frustration toward healing.

You may shed tears of relief as you step from the prison of your own making. Allowing old, repressed emotions to flow makes space for new orientation and life immediately becomes kinder. You encounter people with a new intimacy, warmth and truth. Your fellow human beings are no longer threatening.

This new perception is the truth, it can be trusted. You are an equally important part in the web of Life. You are not alone. You are connected to love. You are connected to Life.

The young soldier

A young woman sat across from me on the train. She was talking to her brother on her cell phone. Again and again, she demanded her brother approve her decision. »Be happy for me. Be proud of me. I did it! Only a few people pass muster.« She went on to describe to him the unit she had been assigned to for basic training.

Eventually, she ended the call and beamed at me. She explained that she had applied to the army and today she has passed muster, receiving a thirteen-year contract. I remarked that thirteen years is a long time. The young woman nodded, yes, that was true, she confirmed. Her decision, she continued with conviction, gives her professional and financial security. She is well aware that we are living in a competitive world. Before she can afford to realize her own dreams, she must achieve something, have something to show for herself.

As it turned out, the young woman was just eighteen years old and completely in the clutches of her ego. Thoroughly integrated authoritative dictates prompt her behavior and decisions. »Before you are considered good and worthy, you must accomplish something, you must gain society's approval. Only then, can you (maybe) follow your heart's desire.«

The young woman had mistaken a collective madness for the meaning of Life. You may recognize the backlash as you read these lines. Following the ego's dictates because you have nothing veritable to compare them with, puts you in great danger of losing yourself completely in complicated, straining and even life-threatening situations.

Reflect a moment and discover in which areas of your life these »I must« voices get loud. They are usually precepts that you have heard from childhood on, from family members and society. They talk you into doing things wholly incompatible with your natural function in this world.

You don't have to do anything. You already *are* and that's enough. Life deemed it valuable to manifest itself as you, in your body. Life chose you. It wasn't your parents. The moment they conceived you, they hadn't the slightest idea that precisely *you* would come of their union.

Life created you and it is only to Life that you owe any obligation. Life created your parents, too, by the way. It was not their doing. Everything happens as it is meant to occur, otherwise it would have happened differently. Without exception. Ergo, you are just as valuable as any other living thing on this planet.

Everything is created by Life, making Life the only authority and the only creator. No matter what you do, you cannot make Life more valuable, nor can you make it less valuable.

Developing a feeling of self-worth purely by the power of your precious existence, you no longer need to prove your worth to the world by collecting socially accepted trophies.

Without consciousness, you are proud of your professional success, status and wealth. Yet they do nothing but bloat your ego. Self-love, benevolence and a profound appreciation for Life are the gifts you receive when you acknowledge your true nature.

I must succeed

»No time to rest. If I rest and tend to myself, I'll never make it.« This is another highly effective thought pattern, propelling us through life, perpetuating the compulsion to charge full speed ahead.

Our barely perceived need for a healthy, new direction is relegated to the back seat, occasionally speaking up at the wrong time, blocking our path and holding us back from gaining ground.

Surely you can recall a moment when you have cursed your physical and mental weaknesses, as they call out to you for a respite? Don't you sometimes wish you were more resilient, stronger, needed less sleep – just so you would have more time for important things? If you are nodding your head as you read these lines, then you are firmly in the clutches of your ego, which dictates what you may and may not do. You are a prisoner of a crippling rational mind and believe everything your thoughts tell you about who you are and what you want.

I recently saw a jogger wearing a t-shirt with the slogan *Punish your Machine!* What did she think her body had done to her to deserve punishment? That is only a minuscule example of the battle most of humanity is fighting – the battle against ourselves; against Life.

The thought pattern »I must succeed« has a related, equally urgent thought pattern just behind it, easily taking hold. »I must gain others' love and appreciation. If I fail to do in this, my surroundings will confirm what I already know deep down inside – I'm not good enough.«

Two childhood thought patterns merge and grow into one vaguely threatening I-must-make-it precept in adulthood, giving the ego high-combustion fuel to drive us hard, harder, hardest. We charge toward goals we believe we absolutely must attain to finally become happy.

But since all these goals lie somewhere in the future, it is impossible to foresee whether they will be realized or not. The ego may plan, insure and take any and all precautions, and still be plagued by the fear of failure, as fear is an integral part of the performance drive. Straddling the fence between hope of success and fear of failure engenders intense inner pressure.

The significance society gives to success, to *making it*, is reflected in a thousand ways every day and everywhere. From newspaper headlines to private conversations with friends, the talk is about how someone has made it, or not. *Making it* usually means attaining material wealth. We rarely wonder about the soul's condition when we speak of those who have made it. Are they equally rich in serenity and inner fulfillment? Or do they merely have a pile of money at the bank, and are now haunted by worries of losing it to scams or to their own inability to invest sensibly? And how long will those who have made it be happy with what they have made?

Especially those who have won their riches over years of demanding work, by overcoming enormous hurdles, realize too late in life, that they have wasted valuable time. In the final analysis, despite wealth and fame, they are still dissatisfied. »What, exactly, have I achieved?«

The answer is, nothing of true significance.

The creed »I must succeed«, is nothing less than a mantra for citizens of industrial nations. A plethora of communication channels brainwash us into believing that performance is the sole purpose in and meaning of life. In reality, we are missing the whole, essential point. Life creates us, but for the millisecond of our time here on this planet, we wrench the steering wheel out of its hands, believing we create life. Yet we have not contributed the tiniest particle to our existence.

»I would like to create something« is mistaken for »I *must* create something.« The natural impulse of human beings to express themselves creatively is supplanted by the noxious thought, »I am not good enough.«

Every one of us longs to be creative. We yearn to express ourselves. Of course, as this is our true nature. Even though we doubt ourselves, we still want to blossom, like a tree or flower.

You may lay a huge stone on top of a tree's seed buried in the Earth. So, what? The tree will find its way around the stone, and grow to be strong anyway. That is the creative nature of trees. The tree doesn't think »I must succeed.«

When we view hurdles and problems as fertilizer Life provides to help us grow, we no longer resist what the moment offers. We are then in harmony with Life.

Something's missing

Do you feel that something is missing right now, or that you must do this or that in the future in order to feel better and whole? Or do you believe everything was better in the good old days, and miss the comfort of the past?

Most people are familiar with the feeling »something is missing.« We take it for granted and consider it normal. But there is nothing natural about it.

This inner sense of lacking expresses itself through our desires in a myriad of ways every day of our lives. We often wish for more. Maybe we wish for more recognition, more money, more material goods, more sex or have the need to eat more than is good for us.

By accumulating *more*, we subconsciously attempt to fill the void we feel inside. We believe that by collecting things from the outside world, we can stop up the fissures in our soul. And sometimes it seems to work, at least for a while. But all things and/or situations pass, fulfilling their purpose only for the duration, and then they are gone, leaving us once more to feel the lack. And this emptiness burns in us. We look outside to the world for a new, universal remedy to soothe our wounded souls.

There is an entire world of variety and material diversity just waiting for us. We could spend our entire lives amassing *more*, while attempting to quiet our longing for inner abundance. This nagging inner vacuum arises from a loss we suffered very early on in our childhood. Our conditioning severed us from the feeling of unity, the oneness we do not or cannot consciously live now, in our adult lives.

As little children, we had everything. Secure in our oneness, nothing could be missing. Life's abundance was who we were, we experienced ourselves as Life itself. Only when we were indoctrinated with the erroneous belief we are nothing but a tiny, helpless body, were we suddenly bereft, lacking all kinds of things. The quest for security and comfort began immediately, because without these two, our lives are threatened.

Our quest for security and comfort continues. It has never stopped, not even for a moment. Again and again, we settle for poor imitations because we keep looking in the wrong direction.

Only in the here and now, in the present moment, can you wholly perceive Life's abundance. Our thoughts, however, constantly catapult from the past to the future and back again. They are incapable of recognizing the present tense. Past and future are mental imaginings, arising in the present – right now – but are completely unrelated to this moment. Thus, it is impossible for thoughts to provide a satisfying feeling of existent, inner abundance. On the contrary, thoughts overshadow the present moment.

We are often obsessed with our past. We either blame our past for our current suffering or we glorify it as a time where life was simpler, less burdened with problems. On the flip side of our thinking and beliefs is the future, that treasure trove of hope that will soon fulfill our profound yearning for happiness. »The moment I go on vacation, as soon as the house is finished, when I retire or win the lottery, then I will be fulfilled.«

Our rational mind promises us a golden future, but we are subconsciously terrified that the future holds misfortunes that will destroy all our hopes and dreams. And yet, many people choose this tug-of war between resentment, worry and hope over living in the present because we feel more at home, safer, in our prison of thought than in a conscious, but wholly unfamiliar life.

Although our thoughts primarily refer to the past or future, i.e. to something that does not even exist, they produce a solid feeling of real identity. Apparently, they stretch a kind of force field that spans from an imaginary past to an imaginary future. This generates a sense of chronology, where an illusory I can exist.

Thus, we lend credence to our inner story-teller. We listen raptly to its empty promises of a fulfilled, future life or spend our time in the past, wishing it had been different than it was.

In contrast, the present offers us nothing to support our self-deception. The present has no need of plans or stories, and that is terribly unsettling. There is something missing in the here and now, namely, our dominant illusory I. Insecure and feeling the lack of identity, we choose to cling to our rational deceptions instead of letting them sail away, opening ourselves to the profound and loving present.

There's not enough to go around

Sometimes we sense the void because we hold the abundance of Life at arm's length. A corresponding thought comes with this feeling, »I feel the lack because there's not enough wealth to go around. So, I am going to make sure I get my piece of the pie, even if I have to take it from someone else's plate.«

Maybe you know someone who is often thrusting herself forward say, »It's my turn now.« The discomfiting emptiness inside of us can not only invoke sorrow, it can also provoke aggression and combativeness. On the outside, such go-getters may appear to be self-assured and goal-oriented, but at the same time, on the inside, they dread powerlessness and are terrified of missing out on what they believe life has to offer.

This dread is a childhood remnant. As a child, an aggressive adult felt his true being was invisible, and how he truly was, was not sufficient by a long shot. If you have yet to rediscover your source of life energy, you most likely think someone else is responsible for your dissatisfying situation. You believe you are vulnerable and can be robbed of whatever it is you strive for.

This distorted mental attitude, that Life creates loss, often breeds egotism, xenophobia and aggression. A jostling, me-first mentality emerges and you, above all others, are the next in line. Remind yourself that no one can rob you of anything.

The abundance of Life is already in you.
In fact, you *are* the abundance of Life.

Bigger and better

Right now, you absorb Life's beauty with all your senses. How can the future provide anything better?

If you should one day live in a huge mansion, you would still only be able to perceive your surroundings with your senses in the present moment. Do you believe that one day, in your luxury pool, you will perceive the water on your skin as something other than water on your skin? Will the expensive wallpaper in your spacious living room trigger something other than an optical impression? You may possibly feel somewhat nobler in your palatial domicile, for a while.

You believe your plans for the future will bring a change in your senses' perceptions. But the future is nothing but a mental concept in your head, the last place to find change. The only place offering sensual awareness is here and now.

If you already have a roof over your head, it makes no difference to your true Self whether you live in a mansion or a studio apartment. The abundance of Life you seek is inside of you and could care less how large or small your home is. You can only sleep in one bed at a time.

If you need more space, if you need new or different impressions, go outside to a park or a forest. Look at the trees, look at the sky. You will realize that taking part in *a* forest is just as delightful as taking part in *your* forest. Are trees more beautiful when they belong to you? Besides, you can't own anything anyway. You already are everything. So, it goes to follow that there is nothing and no one you can purchase.

What may initially sound like unwelcome news, is actually a liberating insight. Since nothing belongs to you, there is nothing you must hold on to; nothing you have to worry about. You can accept and thoroughly enjoy all the gifts Life is offering you without fear of losing them. Look at the colorful world around you. Take pleasure in the fact that it belongs to itself and is there for you all the same. This is the best you will ever have.

Are you seeking the extraordinary in life? Take a look at a blade of grass, at a leaf on a tree, at a flower or a falcon circling in the sky. Can you explain these miracles? Can you fathom their true essence? The thing you are longing for is directly in front of you. The ordinary is the extraordinary, there is absolutely no difference between the two. This is the key to your happiness.

Positive thinking

Have you pasted a small note to yourself in your home with a message that you don't really believe? Something like, »I am self-confident, attractive and fearless.« Do you read this message aloud from time to time? This auto-suggestive technique is called *positive thinking*.

Replacing one emerging thought with another, supposedly better one, is not the best path to take toward self-acceptance and balance. Besides that, as we learned at the beginning of this book, we cannot and do not create independent thoughts ourselves.

Perhaps you believe that new thoughts about your reality, about yourself or about a given situation will change things for the better. But there's a catch. Positive thinking can intensify the friction already plaguing you as it brings you to concentrate even more on your thoughts, instead of striving for mental tranquility.

It is impossible to achieve long-term improvements in the current inventory of your inner life by adding even more thoughts. The present moment *is*, you don't need to correct it.

It could be that you are still being influenced by the lack of self-trust carried over from your childhood. That you have more faith in other voices, such those in a book of affirmations, than the voice of the ever-occurring present, is both understandable and normal.

Still, do not repress emerging, uncomfortable thoughts. And beware of the temptation to try and force them out with other thoughts, no matter how positive they may be. The thought, »I don't want to think that anymore« is an exercise in futility, as it only intensifies resistance against what is, generating even more thoughts.

Develop an open approach to your inner bustle. Accept whatever appears, without judgment. In this way, you find the path to your true essence, which lies beyond thought. Your thoughts will dissolve and you will think less, creating space for inner silence, tranquility and self-assurance.

Old beliefs

Among the subconscious beliefs steering us away from our true selves, there are several that make life particularly difficult by engendering constant self-doubt. We have carried them within us for so long, it is difficult to find and expose them.

Therefore, it is time to shine the light of consciousness on them. An effective antidote is viewing these beliefs from the perspective of your true being. These are neither affirmations nor positive thinking. Taking on new thought patterns will not liberate you from suffering. Freedom comes by naming and acknowledging your true nature.

Belief: I am not loved.
Antidote: I am here and alive because Life chose to express itself through me. Life loves me so much, it wants to experience itself through me.

Belief: I am not wanted.
Antidote: I am here and alive because Life chose to express itself through me. Life wants me.

Belief: I am worthless.
Antidote: I am here and alive because Life chose to express itself through me. Life found me worthy of being created.

Belief: I must succeed.
Antidote: I am here and alive because Life chose to express itself through me. There is no greater success.

Belief: I am not important.
Antidote: I am here and alive because Life chose to express itself through me. Life deemed it important to create me.

Belief: I am guilty and sinful.
Antidote: I am here and alive because Life chose to express itself by creating me in absolute responsibility as an image of itself. Life does not judge. Life knows neither guilt nor sin.

Belief: I am invisible.
Antidote: I am here and alive because Life chose to express itself through me. Life sees me, Life created me.

As you noticed, regardless of belief, the *antidote* is the same. You have been created by Life. You are here and alive. This proves beyond a doubt the significance and worth of your existence. Life loves you and wants you, which is why Life called you into being.

You can neither enhance nor detract from your worth. So, relax, love and appreciate Life, and do whatever you want to do.

Thoughts come and go, that's how we are built. No matter what they say, forego judging them, forego commenting on them, and most importantly, don't take them so seriously.

You might discover other detrimental thoughts, negatively influencing your life. Analogous to what you've read above, you can now develop your own, healing antidote. Remember, what you are has no relevance. Relevant is *that* you are.

Row your boat

You are sitting in a rowboat, crossing a river. Lost in thought, you are brought back to reality when a sudden jolt rocks your boat. You look up to find another boat has rammed you. But the boat is empty. How do you react? Reflect a moment on this situation to see your reaction. Then read further.

You are most likely somewhat taken aback, wondering how an empty boat came to ram yours. Nothing really happened, so you simply continue calmly on your way.

A while later, you come to another river. Again, your boat is bumped. This time, though, there a person sitting in the boat. How do you react? Reflect once more on this new situation. What is your honest reaction?

It's quite possible that you are annoyed and say to the other person sharply, »Watch where you're going! You must have seen me coming!« This is a completely different reaction to the situation with the empty boat. And it is a typical reaction of the ego.

When another person is involved in an unexpected or threatening situation, we feel an immediate impulse to attack him or her verbally. At the least opportunity, the ego is quick to project responsibility for whatever has occurred onto the other person. She or he has caused the calamity. Yet, when no other human being is involved, it is much easier to accept an occurrence. We shrug our shoulders and move on with our lives.

The ego has no idea what caused the two boats to collide. It cannot reach a judicious conclusion because it is not capable of doing so. The ego's primary aim is to latch its insecurity onto a fixed point. This is why we are often incapable of reacting attentively, kindly and fairly to challenging situations.

In the boat scenario, for example, it may have been kind to ask the other person whether they are okay or not, whether they need help. But the ego is rarely out to cooperate. It needs confrontation to boost itself, to solidify its point of view and identity by saying, »I'm right.«

On our little boat trip, you could sense how precisely the ego is fine-tuned to attack and defend. Be attentive in all situations where you become nettled and want to attack your counterpart. Unnecessary assaults and the fury they incur damage your organism.

Life is like an empty boat floating toward you. You can always choose to react consciously and serenely. Choosing not to attack is healthy for you and your environment.

In court

As a rule, defending yourself is considered justifiable, whereas attacking someone has negative connotations. Despite this differentiation, any form of defense is the same as attack. We are seldom aware of this fact, which allows a damaging mechanism to kick in without our knowing it.

A young conscientious objector was summoned before a judge to undergo and sign an examination of his conscience. The judge described an imaginary scenario. »Imagine your family is threatened by an armed intruder. What would you do, if you also had a weapon?«

The young man responded with a heightened awareness, »You are asking me to assume a situation that does not exist. My family is safe from harm. I am standing here in court; the sun is shining and my family is fine.« The judge replied, »Yes, but imagine this threatening situation, and you have to defend your family.«

The young man re-joined, »No. It is precisely such thoughts that bring about conflicts in the first place. The thought, *I must defend myself*, is the initial aggressive act, as it assumes a threatening environment. An alleged opponent is accused of deeds that, at the current moment, have not even occurred. Yet, to forestall these imaginary acts, a defense should be built against them.

This is the epitome of an aggressive mental attitude. The human ego will not cease to attack others because it is permanently fearful of attack. Thus, one person's thought patterns combat against those of another person.

One solution to this conflict is unconditional love. This is the antidote for fear. Since ego is first and foremost a product of fear, veritable love entering an assault situation brings on the ego's downfall. Where there is love, there is no place for fear, just as light supplants darkness.

Thus, from the ego's point of view, its greatest enemy is unconditional love, because love is the most powerful way to dissolve the ego.

Any time we desire, we can respond to our alleged opponents or enemies with unconditional love, which means we witness them as being essentially the same as we are. We do not need to fear attacks, as we are not our thoughts. What we are cannot be threatened. We are completely safe and loved.

The imaginary scenario with my family is an excellent example of our unconscious collective existence, which is the only reason wars are waged.«

If every human being was this conscious, no weapon would ever be fired again.

Bull's eye

When you are involved in a verbal confrontation and your opponent says something that strikes the center of your target, the words have a physical impact. You might become angry and feel thrown off balance. You feel hurt and unjustly accused. Your immediate impulse is to counterattack. Your thought patterns must be defended because, in your rational mind, your opponent's thoughts are simply wrong.

If you were to shed the light of awareness onto this situation, you would discover your error in judgment. An arrow can only hit home when there is a target to hit. Something inside of you responds, or resonates, with the words spoken by your counterpart. When, in contrast, he or she had said something completely untrue, it would have had no impact on your emotions.

For example, she says to you, »You are the most vindictive person I know.« Since you know you are a forgiving person who quickly forgets conflicts, you would find her words perplexing at the most, or even amusing. The accusation or provocation has nothing to do with you and you wonder what in the world she is talking about.

If the words are true, however, without you being conscious of it, you would react quite differently. The criticism's arrow bores into your subconscious identification with being a vindictive person. Your illusory I reacts with denial and fright. It wants to hold on to its more sovereign pose, but the criticism belittles its sense of self-worth.

An ego has countless aspects, countless attitudes and poses. The more aspects you identify with, the more targets you are compulsively driven to defend. And since these inner processes – identifying creates a target; a target is hit by a remark; your defense mechanisms kick in – are subconscious, there are countless situations in which you have the feeling you must defend yourself.

The only time the ego puts aside attack and defend tactics is when it foresees defeat in what it considers to be a delicate situation. This scenario calls for a different strategy, and the ego appears to concede its point.

When one of our targets has been hit by a statement in a discussion and we sense the truth of the assertion, we rarely admit it. We are suddenly no longer interested in continuing a discussion that is sailing into dangerous waters and could expose our weaknesses. So, we bring the issue to a close by quickly agreeing with our counterpart, thus diverting the danger of more direct hits and their corresponding emotions they arouse.

At the same time, a voice inside you whispers, »Let him talk. I know I'm right.«

Behind our fictitious concession lies the arrogance of our rational mind. We outwardly concede, while maintaining a feeling of superiority. This mode of thought and action only serves to further empower our ego.

The moment you acknowledge that you are not your thoughts, conflicts and your dread of assault stop.

Know your targets

Get to know yourself better. Probe your thoughts and emotions to discover where you need to work on integrating issues. Be attentive in situations where you feel offended, hurt or unsettled. In every one of these instances, you have a target. You subconsciously believe that you own the weakness your counterpart has brought into the discussion.

No one can unsettle you by talking about issues you *don't* own. A person can only arouse your dismay by pushing the right buttons. Avoiding that person will only lead to another person turning up to take his or her place. And the vicious circle keeps turning.

There is only one path to freedom from discomfiting situations. When you recognize and accept your defense mechanisms, you can then dissolve them or integrate them into your life. Life does not offer you challenges to make you unhappy. The challenges are there to nudge you toward consciousness.

The next time you encounter an accusation, say, »Yes, it could be that I am like that. And now that I realize it, I may change it.« In this position, you accept yourself and your counterpart's opinion. Thus, the battle of egos is laid to rest.

Collective coercion

A group of philosophy professors meet for their annual congress. One professor reported, »God visited me last night and offered me a choice between all-encompassing knowledge and eternal joy. Naturally, I seized the opportunity and chose all-embracing knowledge.« His colleagues are amazed and beg him, »Tell us! What is this all-embracing knowledge?« The professor replied, »It is the wrong choice.«

When we were children, sitting at the dinner table with our parents, we often heard, or later took part in, discussions on various life topics. Sometimes the discussion became an argument.

As long as we can remember, we have been absorbing opinions and value judgments. Some we rejected, others we accepted as common truths. Constant, repetitive confirmation of a given opinion, from varying sources such as parents, teachers or friends, leads us to believe that »If everyone says it's true, it must be true. I even read it in book or newspaper.«

Surely you have heard the expression, »no sweat, no glory.« And it's true, planning and action are necessary to achieve a goal, which is fine, when the sweat is shed joyfully and enthusiastically, in the conviction of working for a meaningful end. Yet often, in our society, we interpret the phrase to mean excessive labor without joy or pleasure. If what you do is not toilsome, it has no value.

»Business before pleasure« is another axiom implying that enjoying your job is suspicious. We have heard these two widely accepted views our entire lives, in all shapes and sizes, until we finally take them for the truth and now do our part to spread the word.

In the same way, we learn many moral and societal values without ever thinking twice about their validity. In the meantime, they have become an integral part of our self-image, making it even more difficult let them go.

Our rational mind needs a comprehensive arsenal of opinions to be prepared to take a stand, regardless of the situation. Our self-worth depends on having a firm position, because without it we feel insecure.

Our illusionary I, our ego, is a fortress of thoughts. If these thoughts are belittled, the ego feels belittled. To avoid feeling small, the ego stockpiles opinions, preferably socially accepted ones, to have at the ready. This subtle structure is the ego's identity card, making it a full member of society. Sharing the same mindset, there is no need to feel threatened.

Loosely adapting the motto, »Eat more shit, millions of flies can't be wrong«, we not only identify with our own ego, we identify with the ego of a greater majority. We have adapted our belief system and thought patterns to that of a collective, giving us a greater sense of security. Collective behavior patterns and reactions are far more radical and insane than anything our small, individual ego could come up with by itself.

If you are a member of an association, fan club or political party, you have most likely experienced how group dynamics can ferment. Within this social circle, you may have been swayed to do things you would have never done on your own.

A collective has its own yardstick to measure standards and its own value system. Your job as a member is to fulfill these standards and comply with these values. Any dissent on your part leads quickly to conflicts. You may even have to leave the group. Since you feel stronger and less vulnerable in a group, you strive to maintain an advantageous position, succumbing to peer pressure.

Your group may take part in demonstrations for or against a given issue, where you call out slogans on the street. You probably wouldn't do this on your own, either lacking the courage or motivation. Once the collective ego gains momentum, there's no stopping it. It can even come to verbal or physical confrontations with other groups having contrasting standards and values, heightening the potential for aggression.

Sometimes, within the collective, you vent your resentment against your alleged powerlessness. You believe you are right, even though you do not know the original source of your frustration. You only know that you are furious, so you unleash your fury on the first thing to cross your path.

Back at home, when the dust has settled, you may begin to doubt the rightness of your actions, wondering what you have done and why. Uneasiness creeps in, but your ego is quick to explain away any qualms and convince you everything is just fine.

Another example of collective coercion takes the shape of faith in the daily newspapers. There are stories published for critical and intellectual readers.

Intimate details of celebrities' lives are spread over the front page, and with this fragmented information we pass judgment on the person in question. Did she, or didn't she? We don't know, but we certainly have an opinion on the subject, and any other subject, to boot. Our views are powerfully influenced by social and media output. We have joined the ranks of collective thought. Our status, regardless of which social group we belong to, does not allow us to *not* have an opinion.

Both collective and individual identities are fierce in defending knowledge gained through study, literature, conversations with friends or television. We are blind to our inner signposts, propounding a nebulous vision because we define ourselves by what we know.

Oddly enough, vehemently advocating a given viewpoint usually feels exhausting or creates tension. The need to have an undeniable viewpoint is unsettling. But your ego will tell you just the opposite.

A while ago, someone said to me with conviction, »You have to know what is going on in politics and in the world. You must read the papers or at least a few discerning articles on the Net every day.«

When I asked why he needed this knowledge, what was the sense in collecting information, he gave me an odd look. His response came with less conviction than before, »You have to be informed to have your say in the matter.«

This is the ego's attitude, born of the collective conviction **knowledge is power**. If the man had answered truthfully, he would have said, »I have no idea why I need this knowledge, but I can't admit that, because without my knowledge I wouldn't know who I am.« Of course, a person fully identifying with his ego would not be able to make such an honest statement.

Liberate yourself from collective and prefabricated opinions and don't put all your trust in what you know. Trust instead the infinite intelligence of thought-less stillness. There you will find the only truly unshakeable foundation. There, you will experience your Self in the present moment and the insight it brings – your true being cannot be harmed.

I'm right, you're wrong

As adults, our thought content has developed into complex entities. We cling to them fiercely, yet their solidity is precarious and security treacherous, as the concepts we hold and labels we attach to facts and circumstances are not shared by all of humanity.

This difference in viewpoint leads inevitably to difficulties, as our way of thinking is juxtaposed to the concepts of other human beings. This would not be problem if we didn't so thoroughly identify with our thoughts.

»I am what I have learned, I am what I know.« We define ourselves through pieces of paper with our names on them – school diplomas, publications, PhDs, detailed résumés of everything we have done thus far. Anyone denying or questioning the validity of our documented, ink-on-paper achievements, is per se launching an attack on our noble assumed identity. A terrifying act that threatens to annihilate us completely.

Perhaps you can remember a scenario where, for example, you and your counterpart cannot agree on exactly how something occurred in the past. Like a bolt from the blue, the discussion turns into a verbal battle. The original issue is completely forgotten in the face of cutting each other down to size, to see who will come out on top. One of you is right and one of you is wrong. From the ego's standpoint, revising a mental image is unthinkable, as doing so would result in its identity suffering a painful, partial death.

In a fight, both parties are driven by a subconscious mortal fear. Like a duel to the death, both parry contrasting opinions, determined to come out of the battle victorious.

Life is constant change, bringing us new challenges and calling for us to respond flexibly. But the ego is not particularly adaptable. Everything should stay just the way it is, as change threatens the ego's existence. Now you know why varying ideologies and views have so often caused, and continue to cause, immeasurable suffering in the world.

How about you?
Do you want to happy, or do you want to be right?

I haven't a clue

You are having lunch with your colleagues and the conversation centers around a co-worker who was recently dismissed. Some colleagues say they are glad he was fired, he was a trouble-maker and hard to get along with. Others say the exact opposite, claiming it was a pity he was fired, he was good at his job and always spoke his mind openly.

You only knew the man slightly and have little information to go on. Someone at the table asks you your opinion in the matter. How would you normally respond? Would you take sides and enter the discussion or would you honestly admit that you are in no position to make a judgment?

Now look at this situation from the outside. Detach yourself from your body and hover over the colleagues at the lunch table like a spirit. Imagine you don't know the person they are talking about at all. The only information you have to go on is what the people are saying about him. Which side of the discussion is right?

»I haven't a clue« you would probably say. And that is the truth. You can't judge whether the person was rightly dismissed or not because you lack background information.

Observe yourself in a discussion where you are called on to defend your opinion in front of a group. How do you feel inside? Do you feel expansive and serene or tense and limited? The ego, an entity composed almost exclusively of rational thought, is forced to have an opinion. Yet, the moment you express an opinion, you must also be prepared for a counter-opinion, which immediately creates tension. While speaking, you hope your opinion is accepted and reinforced. Up until now, you were most likely unaware of this.

Be attentive when discussing issues. If you have no idea about the topic in question, yet someone asks you for your opinion, reply honestly and serenely, »I really couldn't say.« Even though this may be a devastating blow to your ego, it is the path to your liberation. It won't kill you to say, »I haven't a clue.« Quite the contrary, it will take an enormous load off your shoulders because you are telling your truth.

You also open the way for other discussion participants to suddenly reconsider his or her point of view, and admit that they, too, are unable to make a judgment. What caused this turnabout? The source is easy to find. When you act authentically, the situation becomes authentic. That doesn't mean that everyone is automatically on your side. Yet, authentic behavior often invokes authentic and truthful reactions. And there is no better foundation for communications. Untruthful opinions arising from peer pressure or fear of rejection cannot give rise to authentic encounters.

There are many situations where you can allow yourself to not know anything. Your integrity grants your fellow human beings the freedom to be equally honest and authentic, facilitating easy and open relationships. Our childhood experiences taught us that our verity was rarely seen and sometimes even punished. Thus, we often lack the courage to be authentic, as authenticity is diametrically opposed to our conditioning.

Foregoing judgment is immensely advantageous. Remember – on Life's surface you can only see fragments of the whole, never the whole picture itself. Deep inside, you know these words are true and can liberate you.

What is good; what is bad? What is meaningful; what is senseless? You haven't a clue. Do not judge, do not condemn, it only serves to turn you against this moment in Life. The present. Your ego thinks otherwise. Don't believe it. Feel the profound peace arising from not needing to judge.

»All I know is that I know nothing.« (Socrates)

The meaning of Life

You are good and cherished because you exist.

All other voices may fall silent.

Your being, not your actions, embodies your worth.

You are here because you were meant to be.

Life needs you, it wouldn't have created you otherwise.

You needn't exert yourself.
Life is effortless, flowing easily through you, too,
as an expression of Life itself.

Learn to abide Life's effortlessness.
Even more, accept, appreciate and love it.

Love what you are.
Take pleasure in being here,
in being a part of this multifaceted Life.
No matter which role you play.

Love what is. What is, is all there is.

That is the meaning of Life.

Out of Kilter

You are standing in line at the supermarket cashier. Everyone in front of you has a full shopping cart, but you have only three items in your hand. The line's not moving, no one lets you go ahead of them and the cashier is frantically counting coins into the till. The person directly in front of you forgot some things and runs off to get it.

You notice how your stomach suddenly seizes up and your fingers start drumming on the milk carton.

Impatience.

Lurking beneath this superficial annoyance and tension is helplessness. You feel trapped in a situation that you can't escape fast enough.

Waiting makes you restless because of all those things going through your mind that are so much more urgent. There are many more important things to be done, this moment is nothing but wasted time. But is it really?

It's an opportunity to broach a conversation with one of the other waiting customers. A chance for a pleasant encounter. During this so-called wasted time, you could receive useful information for your private or professional life. Or maybe someone in line gives you a warm smile. And even when all of this doesn't happen, there is still the humming, colorful life around you to observe and enjoy.

Impatience doesn't have anything to do with what is happening right now. Impatience is a rift between the present moment and the inner tumult of your rational mind. And you believe the tension this creates is justifiable. Yet, it is once again your ego's conjectured hustle, bringing on a physical reaction and carrying you away from the present moment to somewhere or sometime other than now.

Biding time

Stop being impatient; stop waiting. Permanently replace the verb *waiting* with *biding*. Instead of impatiently grumbling, »I'm waiting«, serenely state, »I'm biding my time.« You will immediately sense how relaxing it is to simply change your attitude.

Be where you are and bide your time, or do with it what can be done. Accept the here and now.

Besides, along with the potential of standing in line at the supermarket, how could you possibly be anywhere else but here and now?

The scratched shoe

You find yourself in a situation where you could explode. Someone says something that goes against the grain, or you're doing something that just goes wrong, and, out of the blue, heat shoots from your belly to your head and you lose control.

Does this sound familiar? All of a sudden, you're furious. It's a disturbing feeling, but there's nothing you can do about it. You never know when it will overpower you. The same is true for the woman in the following example.

A woman goes to the shoe store to complain about a shoe she had bought there the day before. Annoyed, she approaches the salesclerk, »You sold this shoe to me yesterday. Didn't you see that there is a scratch on the heel?«

The salesclerk defends himself, »Why are you blaming me? I didn't scratch the heel, and you could have checked the shoe yourself before you bought it.« The customer becomes furious, »How dare you talk to me like that! You sold me the shoe! I demand you exchange it for an intact shoe!«

We have all experienced something like this. One wrong word and battle lines are drawn, the verbal combat begins. How did this happen? The customer with the defect shoe feels cheated. Her disappointment triggers a sense of helplessness, followed by anger, possibly tinged with sadness.

But anger is a feeling we neither wish to feel nor to claim as our own. Thus, from the ego's distorted perspective, someone else must have placed the anger inside us. In this case, the customer places the responsibility for her anger at the salesclerk's doorstep, since he sold her the defect shoe.

The two entangled egos battle righteously for the upper hand, as that is where they assume solid ground to be. The combination of creed and anger creates a volatile, emotional mixture. The ego's creed excludes friendly and trouble-free communication.

As soon as you become conscious of this mechanism, you have a choice to react more appropriately. Be aware of aggressive thoughts when they surface, and of muscle tension occurring in your body. Then you know that your conditioning is at work, manning battle stations. You may feel like you want to defend yourself, but as you now know, defending yourself is nothing more than attacking someone else.

Your attentiveness and willingness to forego your own ego games – including the correlating emotions – liberates you from the urge to belittle others. The need simply vanishes.

Once the shoe customer is wise to her inner tumult, she can immediately choose a friendlier tone. She can say, »The heel of this shoe is scratched. Could you give me another shoe please?« Here, she uses neutral language without attacking the salesclerk, leaving him space to react equally openly and candidly.

A conscious use of language results in far fewer conflicts, but our ego needs friction and misunderstandings to bolster its sense of self. The ego feeds on the negative energy generated by raising fences to keep others out, and uses every opportunity to fortify its boundaries. To keep its self-image as secure as possible, our rational mind has but one unchanging slogan – »I must always be in the right.«

The woman in our scenario cannot be consciously held responsible for her behavior. In conflict, the reactionary pattern, of which she is wholly unaware, kicks in automatically. Should she heighten her consciousness, she will enjoy buying shoes a great deal more.

Where anger comes from

Like the woman in the shoe store, anger can be triggered by words or a scenario in which you feel maligned or helpless. Your rational mind talks you into believing you were feeling just fine prior to the situation. Someone else is responsible for your change in mood.

This, however is impossible. No one can open your head and pour in a bucket of wrath. No one can *make* you angry. The alleged opponent merely pushes the buttons that switch on the anger you already have inside you. Be honest with yourself and realize that you *are* furious. And probably have been for some time.

Our upbringing and social standards have conditioned us to reject our anger. We want nothing to do with an emotion that is so negative. We must repress it. »Behave yourself« are words we have heard ad nausea. What exactly is meant, was never clearly defined. Primarily, we assumed, it meant do not be loud, do not be boisterous and for heaven's sake, do not get angry.

Since childhood, you have been wary of your emotions. They caused your parents to give you the cold shoulder. Out of fear of this and other repercussions, you would rather not feel anything at all. Back then, you were fully dependent on your parents and arrived at the following equation, which continues to kick in automatically even though it is no longer true: Expressing authentic feelings = withdrawal of affection and recognition = I will die.

This equation invokes the creed, »Feeling and expressing my rage will kill me.«

Your ego lurks beneath the surface of your perceptions, ever-ready to convince you that acknowledging your rage is equal to a death sentence. Pandora's box must remain tightly shut. You see your wrath as a freakish monster, skulking in the dark, waiting for its chance to pounce and tear you to shreds.

Many of us never had the chance to learn to handle our feelings naturally because no one in our immediate vicinity could, either. It is completely understandable that you fear the power of your anger. You would rather foist off onto someone else the responsibility for your inner tumult, but they usually deflect your attacks. You are trapped inside your fury, have no idea where to vent it and end up as a walking time-bomb, ready to explode at the drop of a hat.

Yet, when you connect with your anger for the first time, allowing yourself to feel it flow powerfully through your body, you will realize just how strong and useful this energy can be.

Consciously released and channeled, using breathing techniques or a form of body therapy, blocked rage transforms into pure Life force. It flows through your entire body, sparking every cell. Nothing terrible has happened.

You did not die. The opposite is true, you have never felt so fully alive before.

Traditional Chinese medicine describes anger as an energy that, when properly channeled, brings about growth, change and creativity. Trapped in body and mind, blocked anger brings about bitterness, resignation, apathy and other disorders.

The word *anger* is merely a one of many labels for a force that can be constructive as well as destructive. For centuries, healers and wise people have known that feelings should never be blocked. They must flow freely, must be an accepted element for Life, in harmony with oneself and one's environment, to be consciously lived.

The emotional realm of a healthy human being is analogous to a bouquet of flowers. Anger, grief and joy, to name just a few, alternate in a constant flow, without rhyme or reason. They are neither repressed nor condemned nor judged.

With this knowledge, you can immediately begin to become your natural and liberated Self. Be happy, when you're happy; be sad, when you're sad; be angry, when you're angry. Trust yourself and allow these feelings to fill you completely. Do not vent them. Don't do anything with them. Be still and attentive and the waves of feeling will eventually fade away.

Heightened attentiveness brings more balance to your inner life. You will experience remarkably less anger and grief.

The cause of your suppressed, and sometimes excessively explosive anger most likely lies in your childhood. Since you were small, you have been convinced you do not deserve to follow your dreams and equally convinced that there is nothing you can do change this conviction. You have borne this powerlessness your entire life. It is the source of your anger and grief, twins born of the illusion that you cannot be the way you are.

In this case, these are not pure, authentic feelings emerging spontaneously, but are emotions triggered by events in your childhood. Such grief and anger usually arises in the context of your ego's errant thought patterns, i.e. when you feel stymied in your movements and intentions.

Thus, an exhausting drama ensues, compounded by the fact that you have thus far denied the natural existence of your feelings. They are blocked by delusional thought patterns that view spontaneous feeling as undesired and threatening. Without being aware of it, in many areas of your life, you feel you have been robbed of your natural freedom and joy.

Until you discovered that your belief in your powerlessness and in your subconscious striving for power was the source of your misleading emotions, you continued looking for the answer in the wrong direction. You became angry at so-called catalysts outside of you.

Take time now to probe within yourself. Instead of a powerless being, you will discover a creative entity connected to a powerful source, ready to serve you in any way. In other words, you are connected to the source and you are the source. The power you have been striving for is useless to you. You do not need power to be happy.

If you do not need power, you cannot feel powerless.
You are free.

Full speed ahead

You are in a relationship and all would be well if your partner wasn't just a tad dissatisfied. Your shared apartment is quite nice, but a house would be even nicer. It's all the same to you; you are content with the way things are and do not feel the need for any improvements. But to avoid a conflict, or bowing under the weight of your partner's expectations, you comply with his or her wishes.

This entails picking up the pace in more ways than one, and you commit yourself to the project. Something inside of you balks at the idea of an additional financial burden, not to mention the added time involved, but keeping the so-called peace at home is more important to you. Your inner voice, speaking to you from the source beyond your thoughts, must be muzzled as you burrow deeper into a new and straining situation.

For a while, things go well and you convince yourself that the new challenge will revitalize your relationship. Your rational mind adds a whole slew of other good reasons for making a change right now.

So, together, you plunge into your new project and are both eager and excited about creating something new. One day, though, you notice that something's not quite right with your body. Maybe you're not sleeping as well as usual or your eye lid has developed a tic or you have an odd, extraneous buzzing in your ears. You pay little attention to these signals, however, because you have other, more important things to do right now. You must carry through with your planned project.

Your symptoms intensify and you suspect they are related to the current strain you are under. But since you don't want to burden anyone and certainly don't want to be considered a failure – in your own or anyone else's eyes – you keep the symptoms to yourself. Come hell or high water, you will finish what you started. You owe it yourself as well as to your partner.

In the meantime, your project is well on its way. It's the worst time imaginable to broach the subject of your growing resistance. Subconsciously, you are following the dogma from your childhood – standing up for yourself is punished with rejection and isolation. You must avoid this, come what may. You have taken great pains to establish personal relationships, yet you also feel that things are moving much too quickly and you need more time to relax.

Your life is hurtling down the fast lane and you simply cannot keep up. You castigate yourself for your need for deceleration. You compare yourself with others and believe something is wrong with you. »Everyone else can manage, why can't I?« You push yourself to the point of total collapse.

This scenario carries both an enormous risk and an enormous chance. Your body's symptoms are undeniable warning signals, admonishing you to decelerate and find your natural pace. If you ignore them, you will find yourself in a vicious circle of illness, guilt and your ego's determination to carry on as if nothing was wrong, to save face. If, however, you listen to your body's protests, you can slow down the enervating pace.

You have every right to stand up for yourself. Your health and happiness are far more important than any plans or projects. This is your truth and no one can contest it. Be courageous, express your truth. You will find that conscious deeds have a positive impact on both your surroundings and on your inner peace.

What's the point in a fine house or well-paid job when the reward is a heart attack or a stroke? Life's joys and inner peace are gifts of the moment right now and can't be found in a non-existent future. You have no idea what life has in store for you. Live now. Don't wait for some imagined, over-riding conclusion to a plan.

Make authentic and loving togetherness a here and now priority. If you're lucky, you still have a choice. Choose now, between subconscious suffering and healthy equilibrium.

When our body talks

Pressure, as described above, often culminates in illness. We feel obligated to a person or situation such as our partner, our parents or our boss.

We often go along with plans that are directly opposed to our need for a time-out, generating significant pressure and tension. Things are moving much too quickly and we feel helplessly ensnared. If we're lucky, our body pulls the emergency brake.

Then, we are forced to slow down. We and those around us must show consideration and make allowances for our battered emotional and physical condition. The scenario we secretly wished for has come about. Driven by our ego, we either weren't aware of our need for rest and deceleration or we refused to admit the need or we weren't strong enough to assert our needs in the face of other's expectations.

When the healthful insight that we are not going to die when we stand up for ourselves is firmly embedded in our consciousness, we no longer need to become ill to meet our need for rest and recuperation. If we are prepared to advocate our needs, we will experience something desperately needed in demanding situations – Self-love. Heeding and experiencing our feelings when they arise is not egotism, it is the unconditional love we have sought in vain from the outside world.

Having lost our natural being in childhood, we now believe that love can only come from someone other than ourselves.

Fortunately, your true entity and the body it lives in, has a much more profound knowledge. This is why your body now sends you unmistakable warning signals, »Look at what you're doing to me. It's time to be good to me and your true Self.« These warnings are often ignored and we believe we must plug on no matter what. But since our true being is much more intelligent than the rational mind, our bodies rebel against the abuse and bring forth intensified symptoms.

Sometimes, when the suffering is heightened to a point where we are forced to get off the treadmill, we come to the realization that we don't want to get back on it. In this case, illness can teach us how to move in a new, more conscious direction.

It can be a gift, as without it we would probably just carry on with our unconscious lives. The illness brings us to make better, healthier choices, to rediscover who we are.

How can I help someone near and dear to me who is suffering a painful illness or is depressed?

This wholly depends on the person's options for confronting the illness consciously.

If the suffering person is averse of indifferent to viewing his or her illness as a chance to bring about change, then there is probably little you can do. Well-intentioned support in this direction is usually turned down.

A certain degree of consciousness and willingness are vital prerequisites for changing, healing and/or integrating illness. A sufferer doesn't have to know what to do, he or she must simply be *willing* to allow changes to take place. If Life intends it to be so, the right paths will open.

Even when the person does not fully heal, the awareness that pain does not necessarily mean suffering brings comfort and alleviation. Despite accepting the illness and all its manifestations, there may still be physical and emotion pain. What will vanish though, is the additional burden of the ego's self-pity and wallowing in suffering. The afflicted person views his or her illness with greater serenity, facing the truth of what is, instead of fighting what the ego believes shouldn't be.

The essential difference in accepting an illness instead of cursing your fate is the immediate comfort it brings. It also helps to view the illness as a temporary condition, and not as something permanent, carved in stone by a diagnosis. A doctor saying, she or he can no longer help means precisely that, the *doctors* can longer provide medical help. Yet Life, who we are, often has a healing card or two up its sleeve for which there is no Latin name.

An ill person's situation can be compared to a prison term. Revolting against our incarceration would have disastrous repercussions. But if we fully accept an apparently inescapable situation, we can find peace and unity in the present moment, despite adverse circumstances. Surrendering to the here and now liberates us.

If you wish to help, the first helpful thing to do would be to accept the situation, and then ask the ailing person what they need. You cannot know why he or she needs to suffer. If you cannot accept the current situation, all your well-intended efforts to help become a battle. But Life manifests itself in a myriad of ways; you cannot fight Life.

We occasionally encounter peculiar explanations for why a particular illness has appeared and what sense it makes. Usually, an esoteric ego expounds, confidently and in detail, the whys and wherefores of a given illness, then stands back and awaits applause. But the ego is not omniscient and is incapable of judging why a person has contracted a certain illness or is struggling with an allegedly negative situation.

Rendering an ego-entangled judgment on why a person is ill is an act of extreme ignorance. It can cause the person who came to us in trust to lose his or her footing, falling into fear and uncertainty, wreaking emotional havoc. Even if you firmly believe your opinion is correct, be still and remind yourself that an *I* cannot judge anything.

One of the greatest challenges for human beings is the confrontation with pain and suffering in our immediate surroundings. We would so like to help and ask ourselves why a person, ourselves or anyone at all must suffer in this life. Life is neither cynical nor sadistic. For some people, however, it takes suffering to inspire them to change direction and open themselves to greater awareness. Still, suffering and illness do not always and only arise to fulfill this role. We will never know why this or that happens to this particular person. This is one of Life's mysteries.

You've got to suffer, to sing the blues

»If I were to do some soul-searching and unravel my entanglements, I would lose my creativity. My suffering, my complicated existence, is my inspiration and the source of my success. Take Beethoven, van Gogh or da Vinci, they all suffered enormously and look at what they created.«

This is a common attitude among many creative people. Yet the belief that you have to suffer to sing the blues is the greatest barrier to true creativity. The source of true, spontaneous creativity is the consciousness of your being – not the illusory I you believe yourself to be.

You are confusing creativity with rampant complicatedness. Only when harmful and complicated ego mechanisms become weaker, finally collapsing completely, do you have the entire potential of Life at your disposal. The origin of Life surges through you with creativity that goes far beyond the dictates of purely intellectual art.

Visit a museum and look at the works of various artists. Some of the artworks touch you in a unique way. Maybe you get goose-bumps or simply can't take your eyes off a picture and stand there gaping. You feel a sense of recognition, as if you are standing in front to a living presence. At the moment of creation, the artist was connected to the source of Life.

Other works do nothing for you, or merely excite your intellect. They do not trigger your amazement, they simply trigger a few thoughts or a bit of praise in your rational mind. These works have nothing to do with art, when we understand art to be creations beyond the rational mind.

Of course, there are artists whose creative process is connected to the source of Life, while they suffer greatly in other aspects of their lives. But suffering itself is neither a prerequisite for nor an attribute of creativity. Occasionally the two come together, but there are far more people on this planet whose suffering closes them off from the creative force. Their inner paralysis keeps them from expressing themselves, despite all their wishes to the contrary, because they are disconnected from the flow of Life.

If you cling to your suffering in the conviction it is the source of your creativity, you limit yourself. Thus, the flow of your creativity may narrow down to a trickle. Turning to your true Self, you will find your creative source and can draw on Life's unlimited abundance.

I'm nothing without my illness

At a table in a restaurant, the guests are talking about diseases. One man describes his soul suffering. He says that despite therapy, he does not have much hope for improvement. He concedes confidently that he now has good reason to believe his disability level will be upgraded from twenty-five to fifty percent, which will increase his welfare payments.

His friend tells of an acquaintance who is in a comparable situation, having also applied for a higher handicap level. When the application goes through, he will be able to stay at home and must no longer cope with growing pressure at his workplace.

Although this approach is not generally true of people with psychological disorders, it occurs quite often. It begs the question, why would some people rather upgrade their disability level to fifty percent than become completely healthy again? Why is the desire to become healthy not even considered to be a viable option?

Humankind is commonly inclined to identify with suffering. People often surrender to what they consider to be a hopeless situation. They cling to their suffering because suffering offers a powerful identity, leaving little space for alternatives. This makes it very difficult to muster the courage and enthusiasm to let go of suffering and seek out a new, unexplored Life.

This is not a conscious decision, but the subconscious defense mechanisms of an anxious ego intent on clinging to what it considers secure.

Should you know someone entrapped in their suffering, forego the temptation to talk them into a better attitude. Of course, you can mention that illnesses are not necessarily permanent conditions, but no one can set out for a healthier life before they have developed the willingness to change their infirm condition.

We are often quick to label such people as weak; they *could* pull themselves up by the bootstraps, if they only *wanted* to. This arrogant attitude has nothing at all to do with kindness. People who are entangled often have one, deep-seated, subconscious thought, »Without my drama, I'm nobody.« They are paralyzed by a latent fear of losing everything they are. At best, the ego imagines a pain-free life, without victimhood, as a void or vacuum, but for the most part, it is terrified of death.

At the moment, it seems a great part of humanity has no other choice than to think and act on their suffering. Maybe the suffering is there to help them grow and finally awaken from the fear-filled world of ego. But only Life can know for sure.

The oven and the spider

There you are, dressed and ready to go with the keys in your hand. You open the door to leave, when the thought suddenly occurs to you that you have forgotten to turn off the oven and coffee machine. You go back to the kitchen to check. Everything's fine, you have shut down the appliances, but you can't remember when and this nags at you.

Going over your day in your mind, trying to remember when you turned off the appliances, you leave your home. Does this sound familiar?

This example is a mild manifestation of unconscious living. You go about your business inattentively and mechanically, unaware of the present moment, unconscious of what you are doing at a given moment.

Not to be confused with the automatic reflexes when driving a car, where such mechanical physical reactions are very useful. All the same, you want to keep your mind on your driving, otherwise you may oversee the pedestrian crossing the road in front of you.

Consciousness is very helpful in everyday situations. It helps you avoid repetitive checking to see whether the oven or coffee machine is off. If you are fully present when you turn them off; wholly attentive in all your daily dealings, you are anchored in the here and now, experiencing every day afresh, and alive.

These mild manifestations of unconsciousness make hardly a ripple in our daily lives. But for those suffering from compulsive disorders, it is a completely different story.

Compulsive behavior is the condition of having to repeat the same action over and over again. A compulsive person's thought patterns are controlled by one, overwhelming thought, »I must do that again immediately.« The ego has taken over completely and people afflicted with compulsions are repeatedly ambushed and taken captive, without any hope of escape.

Yet even this tyrannical ego can be penetrated by insight and awareness when the person gets in touch with present Life. Life has the power to diminish and dissolve even radical thought patterns and behaviors.

There are other examples of subconscious being, where a powerful tension between the here and now and emerging thought patterns is engendered. There can be such an enormous discrepancy between the inner and outer realities, that the body and rational mind cannot cope or react appropriately, resulting in forceful anxiety attacks.

Most of us want to understand, categorize and control our environment, which gives us a sense of security. Yet there are circumstances under which we suddenly lose control. Distorted thought patterns override our control mechanisms, triggering enormous inner tension which becomes visible as phobic or panicky reactions.

Imagine you are sitting comfortably in your living room, reading a book. Suddenly, out of the corner of your eye, you see a movement on the wall. Turning your head, you discover a mid-sized, black spider. Perhaps you shriek and jolt out of your chair to put even more distance between yourself and the monster on the wall. Or maybe you simply gape at the creature, unable to move, paralyzed with fear.

These are typical reactions of those afflicted with arachnophobia. The fear is set off by more than merely seeing the spider. Subconscious thought patterns overlap the actual, current situation. There is nothing terrifying about seeing the spider. The spider is on the wall and you are sitting in your chair.

The parallel thought, however, is wholly other. »The spider is closing in! It is going to attack and kill me and eat me!« Occurring subconsciously, you are completely unaware of this horrifying message, yet its effect is palpable. You automatically react to this subconscious thought pattern with a defense mechanism of excessive fear.

Your ego spontaneously associates the creature on the wall with the words, attack, kill and eat. Your rational mind goes into emergency mode, flashing images and emotions that have nothing to do with the circumstances here and now. Common physical and psychological manifestations are restlessness, breaking out in a sweat, or anxiety and panic attacks.

Immediate relief can be brought about by loudly declaring, **»I will survive this«,** *helping you to recognize that your rational mind is playing tricks on you.*

This may help you to better cope with the situation and is a first step toward integrating the crippling panic and putting an end to your phobia.

Another helpful approach is intentionally putting yourself in situations that provoke anxiety or panic. This is call desensitizing. Here, under professional guidance, you expose yourself to the presence of a spider, learning by new and awakening experiences that a spider is not synonymous with death. In this case, it is recommended to draw on the knowledge of an expert to help you on your way.

In contrast to injurious, phobic reactions, there are natural and sound responses such as the flee or fight reflex when you are confronted with true danger. Let's say a tiger crosses your path in a shopping center. It would be far more sensible to follow your basic impulse to get out of the way than to foolishly invite harm by telling the tiger, »Come on over, I know you won't hurt me.«

At some point, natural, necessary survival reflexes have become falsely associated with situations that have little to do with real danger, giving rise to phobias. This explains why your body reacts excessively when you see a spider.

By learning how your rational mind works, paying less heed to its chatter as well as the emotional and physical reactions it triggers, you disassociate yourself from fallacies and may live free of fear.

Wishful smoking

Is lighting a cigarette one of the first things you do in the morning? Does your day's success hinge on this ritual?

Then you are one of millions who mechanically reach for the pack of cigarettes, going to the kitchen or outside to enjoy a smoke.

After many years, however, there is little enjoyment in smoking, but the nicotine addiction has you firmly in its grip. You have probably tried to quit several times, without success. So, you continue to watch your money and health literally go up in smoke.

But do you really know what damage smoking inflicts on you and others? Aside from the physical damage, the stinking clothes and bad breath, you burden yourself and those close to you with spiritual detritus.

Every time you light a cigarette, there is nothing enjoyable or relaxing about it. With each cigarette, coupled by the knowledge of how noxious it is, you subconsciously relay a message to yourself and the world, »For the next four minutes I have my life under control, even if it costs me my life.«

Those few moments of smoke inhalation and exhalation give your ego a sense of control. For the rest of the time, you haven't a clue as to what Life has in store for you, which is a terrifying thought. By lighting a cigarette, you believe you know what you're doing, at least for the duration of the cigarette. Wild and unpredictable Life is tamed and corralled for the time it takes to smoke a ciggy.

The only avenue available to carry this out is your own body. You probably take better care of your car, if you have one, having it regularly inspected, ensuring it runs smoothly at all times. You might also be quite proud of how well-ordered your life is. Yet, with your body, completely different rules apply.

It's it odd that your car, your home and your clothing are more important than your body. You tend carefully to everything except the temple housing Life. Of course, you feel and know how toxic cigarettes are, even when your doctor gives you a clean bill of health. But you don't really care what you do to your body, or you would stop doing it.

Maybe your self-destruction arises from a subconscious despair because you do not know the whys and wherefores of your existence. In your depths, you no longer wish to live, subconsciously fearing the future. Thus, you could care less whether you live or die. If tomorrow, you should fail to wake up, then you would finally be free of it all. Smoking supports this subconscious death-wish; this attitude so hostile to life.

If you have children and you smoke in their presence, you send them the message, »I don't care about myself. If I had my way, I'd just as soon die.« You may even justify yourself to your children by admitting you are addicted, enjoining them to never, ever start smoking.

Still, you are a role model for your children, sending them conflicting messages. On the one hand, they sense your unnatural, self-destructive impulse, and on the other hand they are completely dependent on you – as described in the segment *I want to be someone else*. Thus, your children absorb your death-wish silently and without complaint.

A young child may not be able to express what she feels, but she knows full well what you are feeling. Fear of Life. And that terrifies your child. »Mum and Dad want to die. What will I do without them?« How does it feel to knowingly inflict insecurity and despair on your children and partner? How do you feel when someone close to you does him or herself damage out of fear or despair?

Can you remember a time when you were a child and your parents weren't getting along very well? Perhaps they were fighting, smoking, or drinking too much alcohol. Whatever it was makes no difference, you can remember how unsettling the situation was.

Subconsciously, you are pervading your environment with the same fear and uncertainty that you experienced and absorbed as a child, along with your blue-gray smoke. How much longer will you bear the responsibility for this vicious circle? Now is the opportunity to break the chains forever by living consciously.

The desire to control everything or, should you fail to do so, to die in the process, is dichotomously opposed to what you are – alive. The ego believes it is a powerless victim. Recognize the fallacy and stop terrorizing your loved ones with your death-wish masquerading as cigarette.

Choose Life.

At the top of the ladder

Our rational minds define success in a myriad of ways, nearly all of which entail having a better status than other people. But what is success? An overflowing bank account? Many children? A perfectly honed body? A lot of sex? Or is success being loved by everyone – perhaps even being enlightened?

Our ego loves and needs to be better, nobler and more significant than anyone else. It wallows in autobiographic stories about itself and its success, telling anyone who will listen, »Look at me, look at what I have achieved.«

Yet when the outer shell crumbles and the stories fall to dust, who am I then? All my efforts were in vain and I stand amid the rubble of my existence. Just a moment ago, I was a successful businessman, a wonderful partner, a perfect mother or father with the reins firmly in my hands. And now, suddenly, it's all over. My success is nothing but cold ashes, I feel desolate and hollow.

This scenario is most terrifying to the ego, then, to be nothing; to have nothing to cling to is synonymous with death. If the ego loses its success status despite all efforts to hold on to it, its sense of self is direly threatened. Clever as it is, the ego then changes its strategy. A new story must be written, a new identity created to which the I can cling.

Thus, victimhood takes the stage, giving me a story to tell myself and my acquaintances, one that ensures a certain amount of affirmation and empathy. »Look at me, look at the raw deal I've been given.« Of course, the unscrupulous financiers are to blame as they took the shirt off your back. The victim's story can take a million different forms, the outcome and ego's intention are nonetheless always the same.

When my acquaintances confirm my misfortune, I feel justified and in the right. The person nodding condolences is a devoted friend. Should he interpret events differently though, having little or no sympathy for my miserable predicament, my feelings toward him can take a dramatic turn.

From affection grows dislike, or even hate. The ego thinks anyone not sharing its opinion and misery is a threat to its very existence. Someone not accepting the gravity and pain of my situation attacks me personally and must be denigrated as a result.

Victimhood refuses to take responsibility for our own life, foisting it off on outer circumstances, reducing us to powerless beings. We believe there is nothing we can do. But we are wrong.

Accept the new situation for what and how it is, say yes to the altered circumstances and act on them to your benefit. By acting, we regain our power. Victimhood is the belief in a thought pattern. It is identification with a story that took place in the alleged past. But every made-up story can only arise in the present tense.

You can choose to suffer, throwing a smokescreen over your present, or to perceive the word *past* in its true definition, realizing that your story refers to something that no longer exists. It is past.

What use is it to linger among dramatic or catastrophic thoughts when you have a delicious piece of apple pie with whipped cream in front of you and the sun in your face?

Although it may look otherwise on the surface, it makes no difference whether you identify with your alleged success or with your alleged failure. Both roles fear letting go of the status quo, fear losing their identity, all the while confusing true identity with a temporary role or function.

You *are not* a teacher, an employee, a parent or an entrepreneur. You only *embody* an impermanent function, which will eventually perish. What you truly are is much larger and much more significant.

In Life, there is no such thing as success and no such thing as failure – these are only the ego's way of defining things. Feeling like a failure is an approach rooted in the past. The compulsive striving for success is an approach projected onto the future. That is how the *I* thinks, running back and forth between yesterday and tomorrow, between resentment and anxiousness.

Realize that the peace of mind you seek can only be found in here and now. Your true identity, veritable stability is right in this moment. It makes no difference which status you hold. Every phase in Life signifies constant change, but all circumstances are striving toward balance. If you can stop resisting change and accept it, you will find your center, you will find peace.

Awaken, an invitation

I invite you to awaken from the nightmare you call your normal life.

You are neither victim nor perpetrator.

Do not be fooled by the imaginings coursing through you. Thoughts do not define you.

Perhaps one of those imaginings has convinced you that you were once misused and so you froze time at that moment, holding fast to your deep resentment. Perhaps you want revenge, or are waiting for a higher power to balance the scales of justice.

This is not going to happen, yet, retribution may be yours. No one has power over you, you can break your chains. You alone have the power to recognize your victimhood and lay it to rest. Be free, and acknowledge your true source of power. Rediscover yourself.

How can a tiny, old thought influence what you are? The past has vanished, stop punishing yourself with this illusion. Let the curtain fall on the dramatic saga of guilt and the guilty. It only plays out in you and Life has no interest in it.

Life is constant change in the present tense, not stubborn clinging to petrified thought-constructs from the past.

What does this moment, right now, say to you? Is the sun shining? Are you having a cup of tea? Are you at home and comfortable? Where are your problems and your victimhood right now, at this very moment?

Look around and realize that there is only this moment and things occur, as they are meant to occur. The sky is blue, because it is supposed to be blue and the sun is bright, because it was meant to be bright.

Everything is as it should be. Why? – Why not? That is Life's secret. We are parts of the whole. Who are we to want differently?

Awaken from your imaginings and take joy in the daily gift given to you. Flowers bloom, birds sing, and expect nothing in return. This, and everything else is there for you.

Say yes to what is, and move on. Life moves with you and welcomes you to Life.

Awaken, you are invited.

The rocky road to spirituality

Our rational mind is a wonderful tool for carrying out practical tasks, for weighing options and for making plans. Unfortunately, this brilliant helpmate is also excessively active and impervious to being shut down.

As we have witnessed, our rational mind is perpetually thinking without contributing much of use to our lives. Instead of listening for answers that surface from a sea of inner silence, we are driven by the white waters of our thoughts. We scamper through life, hounded, with rare moments of tranquility.

Once we recognize this hazardous condition and seek out new paths toward tranquility, our ego launches a subtle, pervasive resistance. It produces a myriad of convincing arguments for delaying change – this is not the time for upheaval, for rest, for new directions.

Should you remain steadfast in your intentions and begin, for example, to meditate, the rational mind weasels its way through to other, cleverer defense strategies. It now praises your decision, affirming your choice method to attain inner peace.

The ego lulls you into a false sense of security, you are pleased and follow your new path joyfully. What you don't notice, is how cunningly your rational mind works to maintain control. It agrees wholeheartedly that you are on the right path, there just a few hitches in the system. Attaining freedom and inner peace takes time. »Just one more seminar and a bit more practice meditating, and you'll get there.« These and similar allegedly supportive thoughts rule the day.

Your ego points to a redeeming future, where all your cares and woes vanish, and you walk faithfully into the trap it has laid for you. Since you have always had faith in your own convictions, you are now certain that a spiritual future will liberate you from your entanglements. What you're missing, though, in your time-consuming eagerness to go further up your spiritual path, is that there is no future; that there is nothing you can achieve at a later date – and your rational mind has led you astray.

Firmly convinced you are becoming more aware, you run from one seminar to the next lecture, read stacks of spiritual books and gradually feel you are an expert in the area. Perhaps you give yourself a melodious spiritual name, or receive one from an enlightened master in a poignant ceremony. You have now completely supplanted your old I for a new, highly subtle, spiritual I. Without noticing it.

Now, when you engage in esoteric discussions, you are well-versed and usually win the upper hand. A sense of superiority is one of the most elementary expressions of the ego, only now it has donned noble, spiritual robes.

Be extremely attentive in this area. The shape a spiritual ego takes is far more cunning than other forms, and therefore very difficult to unmask. Your rational mind is always listening in, is constantly by your side and ever wary. The true quest for inner peace is life-threatening for your ego, so it adapts itself to support your endeavors. An unnoticed, sly spiritual leader.

What do you need more time for and what are you seeking? Do you want to be a better spiritual teacher than the next guy? Such striving only fills the reservoir of ignorance. Do not be taken in by your rational mind's cram-packed bag of tricks, by its survival tactics.

The future is a chimera and holds nothing you need right now. All gifts are given in the present moment. There is no need to travel the world, searching for a redeeming spiritual event, your heart full of holy need.

Be still.

Sit down in silence, and feel what you are now. This is much easier on your health, your appointment calendar and your wallet. What you are seeking, you already are and nothing can change this. Did you, somehow fall out of the divine picture, out of the fabric of being? Are you standing there alone, isolated from all things divine? Even if it feels like that right now – how can you possibly not be a part of Life?

Does what you are need enlightenment? Or is it your ego training for the spiritual gold medal? Then simply say, »I still have an I, but it's enlightened.«

An illusory I strives to be a better illusory I. Realize the fallacy of your intentions. If your spiritual quest brings you much joy and satisfaction, then carry on your way. Otherwise, do not be afraid to attain your goals right now, in the present tense.

The only prerequisites to putting an end to your search are genuine willingness and attentiveness. You may first be confronted with an inner void, as you feel the lack of your fundamental, years-old identification with being a spiritual seeker.

Yet, soon, the void is filled with insight and the awareness of your true being, bringing you the long-yearned-for peace.

Opposition

As you move toward consciousness, you may very well meet with bewilderment among your acquaintances, who do not understand what is happening to you. Their doubt or derision is a subconscious attempt to hinder you on your new path toward rediscovering your true source of being.

There is no evil intent involved here, merely their egos' automatic defense mechanisms, as they feel threatened by your increasing awareness.

An I identifying with troublesome thought patterns feels much more at home with allied egos, preferring to continue wallowing together in the swamp of their lives. The moment someone climbs out of the swamp to see the abundance Life offers, several hands immediately reach up to pull the renegade back down again.

As you become a conscious being, you also become a mirror for your environment. Through you, those around you are reminded that they, too, could approach their lives with more consciousness.

This immediately triggers fear, awakens with a vengeance the old, confining, childhood thought pattern, »I am not allowed to be myself.« Along with this thought, the corresponding repressed pain surfaces. The ego knows and fears this procedure and does everything in its power to avoid feeling its pain.

This situation, in which you wish to express your true self, is analog with your childhood. But this time, friends, colleagues and acquaintances take on the role of your parents, each of them a damaged child, unwilling to feel the pain. The most powerful deterrent in a child's life is the fear of rejection or pain, and the resulting belief that he or she is forbidden to express her or his free nature.

Thus, your striving to break your chains can draw not only opposition in those around you, but also resentment and envy. Your growth indicates to your fellow human beings that taking responsibility for your own Life and allowing essential changes to occur is a viable option. Many will not believe it. They are caught in a double-bind, their own longings have yet to be fulfilled but they dare not express or live them for fear of rejection.

The envious are confronted with their own lack and the belief they are trapped in their unhappiness until death do them part. They may not hinder you on your way, but witnessing your freedom causes them pain, and they turn away from you so as not to feel it. But Life will also send these people indicators, reminding them to move toward consciousness.

Here is a little story depicting a woman's indignation at her friend's choice to become merely a salesclerk, despite her intelligence. She accuses her friend of intentionally circumventing challenges, although she has the talent to go much further up the ladder of success. The woman cannot understand how she can waste her life like this.

She, herself, has gone to great lengths and pains to complete her studies and PhD. There were often times when the effort was too much, and she was tempted to throw in the towel. But her parents were counting on her and expected her to finish what she had started. The woman feels life has cheated her. While she exhausts herself, her friend takes it easy and is apparently satisfied with herself.

The parable illustrates the thought pattern, »If I can't be myself, then she can't either.« Suffering is projected onto the surroundings, which only generates more suffering because it is impossible to permit the fulfillment of one's heart's desires. It is equally impossible to be honestly happy for someone else's happiness.

Envy ferments, but must be suppressed and so, on the outside, one superficially accepts the other's behavior.

On your path to greater consciousness, you may be accused of dabbling in nonsense and wasting your time. And if you are experiencing doubts or anxiety, don't be discouraged, keep to your path. It may be that you are still cleaving to collective creeds that want to pull you back into the fold of homogeneous and socially acceptable behavior.

At this point, it is more important than ever to heed your inner voice, to trust your true feelings more than the clamoring masses. The self-assurance you lost in childhood is slowly gaining ground, gradually being integrated. There may be moments of relapse, when friends and acquaintances distance themselves because they cannot go with you. Don't be sad. These so-called losses will be balanced out, bringing understanding and joy.

A heightened consciousness often brings abundance into your Life. Suddenly, everything falls into place, both personally and professionally. Like a miracle. You are relaxed and radiate joy over Life's generosity, taking only what you need to be happy.

Your authentic serenity reminds many people of their own discontent. Let barbed darts and animosity sail through you. Forgive the critics, they know not what they do, although their petrified ego believes it knows. The consciousness growing in you will become more and more conscious of itself, recognizing coherencies and the all-encompassing unity.

Be flexible

We have absorbed countless unsubstantiated assumptions, judgments and assessments that heavily obstruct our existence. Some we are aware of, and since they appear to give us security by creating solid footing for our ego, we put faith in them, too. But most of these imagined assumptions are simply wrong.

By asking yourself the following question, you can consciously probe the credibility of your assumption on an issue that concerns or troubles you. »Am I one hundred percent certain that my thoughts on this issue are correct?« Listen in for the answer.

Perhaps you would explain your answer like this, »No, I am not one hundred percent certain, but nearly so. So, my assumption is probably right.«

That is the ego talking. A true answer would be, »I don't know if my thoughts on this issue are true.« This is true because the ego simply cannot accumulate all the aspects of a given issue in order to make a genuine judgment. The ego can only grasp fragments, but not the whole picture with all its coherencies. As long as we identify with an I, we cannot possibly be one hundred percent sure of anything.

With the one-hundred-percent-question you create inner space, where new perspectives and decisions on various Life issues expand your options. This is enormously beneficial. It invites flexibility, a must for feeling at home in our constantly changing Life. The ego has no interest in flexibility. »Try something new? No, thanks. New is scary.«

Occasionally you meet someone who appears to be sedate and flexible. He often agrees with you when discussing issues, although he doesn't really think the same way as you do. He just wants to be left in peace. What at first seems to be a friendly approach turns out to be the ego's strategy to avoid changes and maintain its unbending opinions.

Joy, grief and anger need a natural channel of expression. When the channel is blocked by the ego's rigidity, strong emotional energies are repressed and turn against their owner. Repercussions of an unconscious existence could then be tension, pain, depression, auto-immune disorders, tumors and other illnesses. What is this channel? Simply to feel these feelings without wanting to change or alleviate them. And to feel them fearlessly.

Unbending people are not responsible for their condition. When there is no space for developing awareness for one's inner workings, it is literally impossible for changes in thought, word and deed to occur. Yet the suffering may one day cause the ego's armor to rust and the resulting consciousness leads to an improved quality of Life.

Be attentive to what goes on around you and how your thoughts and emotions react. You will quickly have formed an opinion about a given situation. If you are unsure whether your opinion is accurate, ask yourself the one-hundred-percent-question.

An open, caring and non-judgmental attitude changes you and the world, bringing more serenity and flexibility.

The parable of the staff and the bamboo

»Resistance and tenacity are strengths, yielding and flexibility are weaknesses.« This common, collective delusion transforms Life into strenuous toil, it drives us to battle against the ever-present here and now.

Our upbringing and society condition us to believe that compliance and gentleness are cowardly attributes. Determined not to lay ourselves open to manipulation, we at some point decide to confront all Life's challenges with adamant rigor. A decision that robs us of the ability to assess each approaching situation individually, attentively and consciously. By mistaking true strength for weakness, we invite even more unpleasant challenges.

Imagine Life's wind roars at you, hard and rough. If your inner posture is unbending like a wooden staff and you feel strong, you will eventually break under the wind's constant pressure. Just one crack, and body and soul are damaged.

If you are elastic like bamboo, you will bend, even with the most powerful opposing wind, for as long as the wind is blowing. You remain intact, capable of acting, and the moment the wind falls, you spring back, as if nothing had ever happened.

Offer no resistance to what already is, and you will stay strong and healthy. Accept the moment, act with circumspection and a healthy dose of flexibility, and you will remain intact throughout Life.

Return to the Center

At the age of twenty, give or take a year or two, we are champing at the bit, feeling our oats and raring to go. We believe we are free, invincible and ready to take on the world, fully unaware of the old chains we carry, bolted to the walls of our conditioning.

The chains tell us, »I must find love and recognition, otherwise I will not survive.« Had we merely concluded, as young adults, that we have escaped our parents and no longer rely on their affection for our survival, we would have broken the chains of this thought pattern. Unfortunately, the chains are well-oiled, holding us without our knowing it. So, we carry on in the belief that we must contort ourselves for the love and acknowledgment of others.

Our rational mind subconsciously sends the message, »When my boss or partner doesn't like me, I will die.« As dramatic as this may sound, it is a very real drama with millions of people subconsciously playing it out every day of their lives in both their professional and private relationships.

Observe how you react when a person of authority, perhaps your boss, requests a private talk with you. You may become nervous and your palms get sweaty. Even such mild symptoms express your ego's mortal fear.

Unbeknownst to you, the encounter with your superior has little to do with the issue at hand. In truth, your inner program is only concerned about the impression you make upon her. Does she still appreciate you or do you have to make more of an effort to stay in her good books?

These and related questions usually go unnoticed as they course through your rational mind throughout the day, maintaining your dependency on so-called authority figures. You feel insecure, as decades of indoctrination have you believing you are not good enough as you are, and must remodel yourself to survive.

You go to the meeting with your boss full of preconceived ideas. If your employer seems to share your opinions – your thought patterns – you're in luck. Your definition of yourself and your world is confirmed. You can relax your guard as the danger of attack has apparently passed.

If, however, your employer has a differing opinion, the picture changes radically. While you identify with your thoughts, your boss wants you to assume her thought patterns. Tension is inevitable.

What you think should now be replaced or supplemented by what your employer thinks. For you, this is synonymous with replacing or supplementing you yourself. You feel impotent and may become annoyed, controlled by your ego's terror of being erased. Under the influence of subconscious, reflexive reactions, it is not possible to act freely and with self-confidence.

Your employer acts on the same, subconscious control mechanisms of her ego, having the same fear of annihilation. But since she is in the apparently stronger position, your feeling of impotence is more powerful than hers.

It is likely that you feel this impotence in several areas of your life, doomed to an existence of powerlessness. Your suffering, however, has nothing to do with the concrete situation, your discomfort stems from how you think about it. Your interpretation of the world and self-definition are unsubstantiated mental assumptions that have nothing to do with who you are.

You may have never had the opportunity to develop and maintain a natural self-awareness because your parents never had the opportunity, either. Where could you have possibly learned self-confidence?

To get off the merry-go-round of impotence and fear, you need to remember your true being. Each and every conflict you enter is based on the same fallacy, »I am what I think about myself.« Discover what you really are, and you will have found the key to your liberation.

Resistance

You may be a person who is determined to defy life's adversities. You wish to prove that you are not someone to mess around with, someone who refuses to go with the flow. Therefore, you have decided to resist and battle in all areas of your life. You may fight for your rights and for justice, for your relationship, your job, for your money, for attention and for praise. You make a heroic effort.

Read the last sentence again and perhaps a light will go on in your being. You are only a hero in *your own eyes*, and bear the burden alone. Hardly anyone else is interested in what you do or in what you are fighting for, they are much too occupied with their own battles, with their own heroic efforts. They simply haven't the time or inner space for your issues.

So, who is going to give you their full attention after the meeting or telephone call? Only you, trying to prove something to yourself. For whom or what are you fighting? Why make it hard on yourself, when you can have it easy?

It's quite possible that there are issues in your surroundings that annoy you. You have a choice. You can either continue to rail against them, or do yourself a favor and surrender your resistance. That doesn't mean you have to put up with ignorance, without saying a word. A well-placed, distinct 'no' is just as much a conscious act, as long as it comes from an inner stillness.

You may shape your Life any way you like. Life does not require the permanent strain of heroic effort. An old, childhood survival strategy has turned you away from this awareness, manipulating you into believing, »I must fight for my survival.«

The moment you get wise to your ego's tactics, and are willing to lay down your arms, you move from the role of impotent warrior to a place of empowered peace. You lose your abrasiveness and regain your vital energy and freedom.

Be courageous, be loving
and end the war against Life,
against what you truly are.

Should and have to

As you can see in the above example, the illusion of having to do something can generate enormous tension and strain. There is another word which can create just as much suffering.

Imagine you have been at your job for many years and you think, »My boss should finally raise my salary.«
   The reality is, you have been working here for a long time and your employer has yet to raise your wages. At the present moment, reality is shaped as such that your boss has *not* raised your salary. So, what use is the opposing thought, he *should*?

Close your eyes and perceive what reaction is triggered when you think the sentence, »My boss should give me more money.« Do you feel pressure, tension or constriction? Perhaps sorrow? Can you feel what this sentence provokes in your body? These reactions prove the fallacy of your thoughts.

Now, compare that thought with this one, »My boss does not pay me more money. That's the way it is.«

Do you sense a difference? Do you feel a slight sense of resignation that is nevertheless more authentic than your body tensing up? Or does the thought even cause you to relax?

If so, you have caught the scent of your truth. Thus, you can perceive how truthful thoughts, compared to deceitful thoughts, affect your sense of being.

By accepting things as they are, you immediately feel stronger as you now have concrete choices for dealing with them.

Either change the situation, if you can, leave it or accept it completely. Battling or bending reality by dint of your thoughts is impossible. It is a form of the ego's arrogance and evokes only unhappiness and strain.

If the above scenario with your employer has no relevance in your current situation, repeat the exercise with a pertinent statement. Perhaps you are convinced your partner should most definitely do a certain thing for you. By perceiving your body's reactions as described above, put your mental images relating to this scenario to the truth test.

Realize that no one *should* or *has to* do anything for you. That is especially true for yourself. Although inner voices loudly protest the contrary, they are not telling the truth. They are echoing opinions from so-called authority figures that you absorbed and took for your own in younger years. You probably believed that your parents, teachers or acquaintances knew more about how the world works than you did.

As a result, you have integrated unsubstantiated creeds and compulsions into your system, calling these extraneous voices your own.

The conflict arises when the thought, »I have to/I should do such and such«, leads you to believe you can change the present moment. But this is impossible and deep down inside you, you know it.

Sometimes you feel like a failure because you have to do something, but simply cannot. Still, you hold tight to your deceitful thoughts since they are a part of your illusory I. You assume the resulting suffering and strain are merely part of the process and inevitable.

Experience how you feel when you replace the words **should** and **have to** with words such as **may, might, can, could**, or **want to**.

Here are two examples.

Think, »I still *have to* take out the garbage.« How does it feel inside you?

Now, think, and compare your feelings, with the thought, »I still *want to* take out the garbage.«

Think and reflect on the thought, »I *have to* go to work.«

Now, think, feel and compare with, »I *can* go to work.«

Do you perceive the completely different energies in these sentences? For the next week, strike the words *should* and *have to* from your thoughts and speech. If you notice your attitude toward people and situations has changed and become more tolerant, then strike the words *should* and *have to* permanently from your vocabulary. Adopt the use of *want to*, *can* and *may* instead.

By losing two small words, you gain a generous portion of freedom, respect and love.

Carte blanche for everyone

Imagine reaching for an exquisite inkwell and quill. On a piece of silky sheepskin, you write the words *Carte blanche* in large, elegant calligraphy. There is but one sentence below, »You should not and do not have to do anything for me.«

Now sign your name and roll the sheepskin, handing it to your partner, your friends and anyone close to you. How do they react when reading your message?

I bet you can already feel it. The recipients may at first be somewhat taken aback, but when they grasp the deeper meaning of your words, they will be happy and thank you.

Keep one of the scrolls. This is for you. Read the words once more in your mind's eye and take their meaning to heart. Then, it is important for you to know that the Carte blanche you just wrote applies first and foremost to you.

Only when you have accepted and integrated its meaning, can you release other people from your demands and expectations. You can, and may, do this.

A supportive dialog

The following dialog can lend additional support in liberating you from the concepts of should and have to.

»Would you like grass to be blue instead of green?«

> *»No, why should I want that?«*

»Would you like roses to have polka-dotted leaves instead of red ones?«

> *»No, why should I want that?«*

Do you take pleasure in how the rose blooms, or should it bloom differently?«

> *»The rose is fine the way it is. It doesn't need to be different.«*

»How does it feel to allow the flower to be as it is?«

> *»It feels right, expansive and free.«*

»How should your partner be?«

> *»My partner should change who he is, because I don't like some things about him.«*

»What do you feel when you say your partner shouldn't be the way he is, that he should be the way you want him to be? How does that feel inside you?«

»Something constricts inside me. It feels tight and narrow.«

»And how does it feel to allow your partner to be the way he is. Is it like the rose?«

»The constriction relaxes, everything expands inside me.«

»Which of these feeling is more truthful?«

»The second. My partner may be the way he is. That is truer, even though it's still difficult for me to say so.«

»Have you found the answer to how your partner should be?«

»Yes, I believe so. Yes, I'm sure of it.«

These helpful questions offer another opportunity to probe your body's sensations and discover the truth of your judgments and opinions. Feelings bring you closer to your inner being than thoughts do because they are more honest than our imaginings.

When you read a job offer in the newspaper or just come from a job interview, you usually have a gut feeling about it. Either you sense, »Yes, that's it« or »No, that's not the one.« Rely on this inner compass more than on the unsubstantiated assumptions of your rational mind. This makes it easier to recognize things in Life that correspond to your true being, instead of being driven by the belief you have to or should do this or that.

While feelings are good signposts, pointing you toward a conscious and healthy Life, emotions have a different impact. In contrast to feelings, emotions emerge simultaneously with mental imaginings, seemingly confirming and intensifying them.

This noxious process can trigger truly crippling aftermaths. Yet, by probing our thoughts, heeding our bodily reactions to them, we open ourselves to new avenues of action. Our bodies' perceptions lead us down the right and healthful path.

I can be as I am

In your true nature, you are as Life created you. Allow yourself to live your genuine being, and impotence, grief and rage will vanish. You will have more compassion for yourself and the world.

Therefore, tell yourself occasionally, »I can be as I am.«

Soon, you will no longer need the sentence, as the world is once more a friendly place and you have come home.

Relationships

Everything is supposed to work the way we imagine it to work. Our professional life, our surroundings and most of all, our relationships must give us what we so desperately want – fulfillment and security. Oddly enough, it is rarely our relationships that deliver on a long-term basis.

Newly in love, the world appears reborn. Our partner is perfect; everything we have ever dreamed of in a mate. When together, we feel safe and occasionally even cherished. There are moments of profound intimacy, when we shed our masks and become who we truly are. We believe we have found true love.

Yet, after a while, the relationship and partner begin to fall short of our expectations. There are spats, usually over trivialities and our partner reacts differently than we imagine him or her to react. Our love sours, turning from irritation to testiness to outright anger.

How could this be? Can love suddenly turn into anger or hate?

Of course not, true love has no opposing emotion. What is happening here has nothing to do with love. It is the meeting of two needy people, two beggars, who believe the other is hiding something in her or his pocket that the other simply must have.

The subconscious chain of thought runs more or less like this, »You belong to me. You have something I lack. Now give it to me and be the way I want you to be, don't change. Then, everything will be fine. That is my love for you. Don't you dare change. If you do, my love will become hate because you have disappointed me.«

Possession, need and privation are frequently mistaken for love, which is why our relationships are often so difficult. Before we have found the source of true abundance in Life, nothing will ever be enough. No partner, no wealth, no fame will stuff the cracks in our souls.

We didn't plan to be this way, we and the greater part of humanity, find ourselves in a collective, subconscious conviction that something is missing in our lives.

Our perception of love is linked to a feeling of deficiency. A feeling that is difficult to unveil and dislodge. It takes a certain level of attentiveness before we are conscious of our inner processes. Only then can we begin to act for our own sakes.

Once we set out for the source of our true abundance, the needs and expectations we once clung to fall away as we recognize their meaninglessness. When our sense of isolation dissolves, compassion and love emerge in the knowledge that everything is unified and connected.

True love can only be experienced in complete fusion. How and to whom can an isolated individual extend love?

Love's natural aspiration is to freely unfold and expand. When love is not allowed to grow, grief and anger take hold. We often wish to give our love to others, to give them joy or to receive love in return. Our longing is often the seed from which our children are born or our circle of friends grows larger and larger.

A helpful reminder points out another fallacy – it is impossible to give or receive love. Love encompasses everything, it is the core of every being. We do not *have* love, we *are* love. Love begets love in living things. When we recognize someone as essentially and perfectly one with us, this unity is living love.

When we cannot have children, there is no need to grieve. Recognizing our unity with all other living things, we find the world is full of possibilities to perceive ourselves as love.

In a truly, loving relationship, you cannot possess anyone and you cannot be deceived. The only existing deception is your own self-deception, believing you can possess someone. This is not *your* partner, he or she is *a* partner sharing your Life in this moment.

All-encompassing love knows neither need nor possession. Say to your partner, »I do not need you, but am profoundly happy that you are here.« This speaks of authentic love, creating genuine freedom and genuine unity in your relationship. Feel and realize that veritable love is unity and has no opposite.

Good intentions

Perhaps we have been together with our partner for many years. We are familiar with every one of her or his idiosyncrasies and believe we can foresee his or her every move. If our partner suffers a crisis or behaves differently than we imagine, we feel relatively certain we can help them. We think, »I know what my partner needs.«

We couldn't be more wrong. There is a saying, »The road to hell is paved with good intentions.« We cannot know what our partner needs, even if we're together for a hundred years.

Maybe you know the phrase, or one similar, that is whispered to a friend behind your hand, »You just have to nudge him (or her) in the right direction.« This reveals the boundless arrogance of an ego without the slightest clue about authentic relationships. The phrase has nothing to do with brotherly or any other kind of love. How can we possibly assess another person when we don't even know ourselves? We cannot detect our own, true being in the illusory I's jungle of distorted thoughts. As long as we're trapped in the delusion, we cannot recognize or judge anything.

Of course, our desire to help our loved ones shake off a bad mood or rise out of what seems like a negative situation, has only the best of motives. We rarely succeed because our good intentions are infiltrated by a subconscious plan to relieve sufferers of their responsibility for their own lives. And we can't, no matter how much we would like to.

Each and every human being encounters precisely the challenges in Life that are meant for him or her. They wouldn't happen otherwise. Some people recognize the challenge and rise to meet it, learning and growing through it. Other people need a life's crisis in order to develop; a crisis which nearly shatters them.

Regardless of how Life's challenges reveal themselves, their purpose is to lead us to more consciousness. Life does not want to spite us, nor does it want to make us happy. Life wants us to become more conscious. Since every person has her or his own, singular path to awareness, the shape and access to this path is made but once. This is why we rarely understand why this or that happens to precisely this or that person. It is as it is.

Be there for your loved ones. Be supportive, be helpful. If appropriate, ask what they need, without pressing methods or remedies on them that *you* believe to be most effective. You are not a prophet, so throw away your crystal ball and replace it with openness and loving acceptance of the person and situation. This is the best help you can offer.

Brotherly love

»Love your neighbor as yourself.« Who doesn't know this famous quote?

Although we all have an idea what these words mean, how to go about acting on them is less straightforward. It is difficult to overlook another's failings, even more so to accept them. A greater challenge is to develop love for yourself.

Making the above quote a reality is a matter of putting it in the right order. A more practical rendition would be, »Develop love for your Self and you will then be able to love your neighbor.«

We all have some characteristics that we don't like, so we reject them. Yet, by dividing ourselves into categories of good and bad, we cannot give ourselves unconditional love. How am I to accept my neighbor when I cannot accept myself? Is it enough to love my neighbor a little bit? Can love be measured?

No, love encompasses all things. Love is just another name for your true Self. Love cannot be cut up like a pie. If you deny one single person love, you deny every human being love. You deny yourself love. What you call love is only your dependency on attention and recognition, and the fear of not receiving them.

Rejecting one single aspect of Life means you reject all of Life. Life is one. All-encompassing love can only emerge when you wholly accept yourself, including your so-called negative attributes. This means allowing all emerging thoughts and emotions without resistance.

Everything you perceive exists in this moment. All events occurring within you are reality, so it would be crazy to negate or reject any of it.

Yet, day in, day out, our ego does precisely that, creating tension, worry and suffering. The old creed, »I must do more«, puts you under enormous pressure, while the other creed, »I'm not good enough«, traps you in a constant state of impotence and inferiority. But you are here and alive, ergo you can be how you are and who you are. Accept that, and Self-love will begin to flow.

Acknowledge yourself in your entirety, dispense with judging what you have always called failings. It's not difficult. Life has already accepted us. But how can we be sure? Easily. What Life has accepted, exists. And you are here.

This certainly does not mean you have to tolerate your current condition if it doesn't suit you. A loving approach to the situation and yourself makes change not only possible at any time, it makes change probable as you walk the path to sentient insight.

Simultaneously, you allow your fellow human beings to be as they are. They become a mirror in which you can easily find yourself.

There is no longer any need to attack or to judge. This is true Love.

The heart's desires

A while ago, I was sitting in a café with an acquaintance and I asked her about her heart's desires. She replied she would like to expand her business, so she desired more customers. That would be fulfilling.

I sensed she was not really convinced by her own statement, so I asked her whether she longed for something else. Perhaps she had an inner image, one that occasionally, but repeatedly, arose. Maybe an image carried over from her childhood.

My friend became quiet and her eyes filled with tears, as she replied, »To be honest, I wish I were living somewhere close to water, with a family of my own, no longer running in this rat race.«

This was a completely different answer, arising from her true Self. Our upbringing and social environs have conditioned us to relegate our heart's desire to the back seat, where we eventually forget them. But they do not forget us, and reside inside us to this day.

Take a moment to reflect. What are your heart's desires? We're not talking about a new car, a winning lottery ticket or a beautiful partner. Those are all egoistic trappings and will not fulfill you.

Ask yourself, »What is my true longing?« Now wait in silence. Perhaps an image or a memory arises pointing you in the direction you would truly like to take. Probe deeper. Be kind, open and courageous. Your heart's desire may have been buried in the depths of your being for many years. So, inviting it to reveal itself often gives rise to grief or anger.

When you yield to these feelings and allow your deepest desire to come to the surface, you will suddenly experience joy. Later on, as you relate your heart's desire to friends, they will witness the new light in your eyes.

Since childhood, you have probably striven to meet the demands of your surroundings, putting your own desires on the back burner. Now, you have the opportunity to fulfill your dreams. As you strive to fulfill your true goals, Life will support you with all its power. Impotence vanishes, along with grief and anger. You also say goodbye to the feeling that life is your rival, begrudging you everything.

The moment you set off for your heart's desire, you realize you have nothing more to lose. You encounter Life's abundance. And perhaps a few other wishes are granted along the way, but your happiness no longer depends on them.

Traveling companions

Our longings and heart's desires are often obscured by the conviction that there is no space for our true Self. We are afraid of being stymied or punished the moment we begin to express ourselves authentically. There is nothing to fear. Life lends us support along our natural path to self-fulfillment.

Should you choose to turn your energies toward attaining your dreams, you don't necessarily have to give up everything near and dear to you. You can keep your relationships, your job and your possessions.

Necessary for change is inner breadth and width, an open space where innovative ideas for your private and professional life can take shape. Your true needs, and the creativity to meet them, arise more fluently from quietude than from your daily bustle. Therefore, it is very helpful to set aside some undisturbed time each day when you can discover the space and stillness within you.

You may integrate your newfound Life's wish into your daily life step by step.

Look around you, and you will certainly find other people who have, like you, set off in a new direction. Perhaps you can visit a seminar or meeting that sparks your interest. Such 'traveling companions' can provide you with many fresh ideas and valuable information. Common interests, ideally coupled with growing consciousness, are a strong, empowering, joyful source of inspiration.

Trust your feelings on this road more than clever thoughts. Your ego has plenty of excellent arguments against fulfilling your heart's desires, most of them, in essence, chanting the time-worn creed of repudiating conditioning, »You may not be yourself.« This is an antiquated, childhood program and wholly untrue. It is useless. Turn it off, if you can, and if you can't, be yourself despite it.

Remind yourself of your true nature – You can be yourself.

Beautiful, horrible Life

Everywhere you go, on TV and around the coffee table, people are discussing why this or that catastrophe occurred, whether politicians have made yet another mess of things, and how the powers that be have once again cheated the masses.

The most common question posed is, »Why is there so much evil in the world?« The answer is, »Why not?«

That might sound alienating at first, particularly as the existence of »evil« in the world doesn't jibe with our beliefs in God or fate. So why isn't the world simply and completely good?

Every single minute, the world is not only what we call ugly, but is also beautiful. Without asking for anything in return, we receive a unique gift every moment of our lives. The sun shines and warms us, rain falls and nourishes the Earth, making her fertile. We receive smiles, the sofa welcomes us without a word of complaint and tea tastes wonderful. Just because. All the same, you rarely hear someone asking, »Why is there so much beauty in the world?«

We take pleasurable things and circumstances for granted, seldom responding to this generosity with a simple »Thank you.«

Should someone ask me »Why is there so much beauty in the world?« My answer would be the same, »Why not?« Everything we perceive on this good Earth, takes place for a reason – but not a reason we can grasp. This is very difficult for us to accept since, from our youngest years onward, we have been drilled to find a reason for anything and everything that occurs. We are driven to control simply everything. And yet, everything is as it is. This is the simple truth.

Separating, defining and categorizing all things into good and evil is the complicating, distorting, isolating chicanery of our ego – determined to keep us from discovering truth.

»Why then, tis none to you. For there is nothing either good or bad but thinking makes it so.« Hamlet Act II, Scene2. (William Shakespeare)

The piety trap

The ego has a habit of blaming other people for its personal fate. If this proves unsatisfying, there is always the ultimate perpetrator responsible for our misery – God.

Many religions have happily transferred personal responsibility onto the God they represent. They tell believers, »Yes, you are right. It is all in God's hands.« Quaking in awe, we fail to see that this God, according to His representatives, is depicted as an individual, isolated authority with human-like characteristics.

Some religious institutions have long known that our rational minds are programmed to separate everything into positive or negative categories, and use this knowledge to maintain their power, manipulating their followers. For centuries, we have been taught, »This is Good and this is Evil.« We nod in agreement, comfortable with the concept because it is precisely how our ego works – perpetually judging. But as you wouldn't dare to put yourself on the same level as God, Jahveh, Allah or Brahma, as only They, and their representatives on Earth, have the right and privilege to divide the world into good and evil.

At some point, you may have willingly transferred the responsibility for your life onto your God, honestly striving to follow the doctrines of your religion. Yet, eventually, you discover you have difficulties understanding by which rules, exactly, your God governs this world. Why does He allow so much evil to exist? Why doesn't He intervene as you so desperately believe He should?

And sometimes, when you commune with your God, an uncomfortable feeling creeps over you, without your knowing why. You are unsettled because you do not know what will happen to you when you die.

Subconsciously, your ego is convinced it does not deserve divine redemption, since it is in constant conflict with your true nature – Life itself. Still, you hope and pray that you will not be doomed to perdition when you die.
But redemption is also frightening, since death and redemption mean the same thing in your thought system.

Life, your true nature, often appears to you as a threat. So, you put your faith in the 50:50 chance of a carefree life after your so-called death. You swap your fear of Life for your fear of death. Can you see the madness behind ego-driven piety?

Believing in a far-away God, holds us trapped in a life equally divided between hope and fear. Have you noticed that the word »hope« itself is deceiving? The word hope includes the fear that our hopes will not be fulfilled. If hope were dressed in fearless robes, it would be called trust or confidence.

Without being aware of it, you have been downright traumatized by your religion, but believe this condition is normal, or even desirable. And, of course, your religion is the one true faith. Excluding or segregating breeds exclusive or segregated thinking, making true unity a very slim possibility. Adhering to prescribed dogmas of a religious institution means adhering to the insane collective ego, which sees unity as a threat.

It is often said, »My faith is my support.« Subconsciously we are saying, »My faith is my identity.« Observe the double use of the word »my« in both statements. The collective religious image has become my own self-image. »Where would I be without my faith? What would be left of me? This is a terrifying thought, so please don't plant doubts in my faith.«

Where does the belief in a single God come from?

When consciousness identifies with a human existence, it feels isolated, cut off from the unity of all things. In our need for divine support, we project the delusion of our isolation onto a single, isolated, hyper-dimensional God.

The inadequate human ego creates a being in his or her own image, bestowing upon it superhuman attributes such as omnipotence, omniscience and unlimited mercy. And then, in our despair, we ask this Super-Being why it created suffering, disease, poverty and war.

The moment consciousness liberates itself from a personal I, we understand that there is no separation, there is no such thing as isolation. There is only a single, coherent Oneness. Thus, the belief in a distant God, leading us and judging us, crumbles to dust.

As long as we are controlled by our egos, we will not be able to develop and perceive an all-encompassing sense of being. Of course, we can always imagine an omnipresent God, penetrating all things. But when our need is great, we once more feel thoroughly isolated from our God, who is an equally isolated being. Still, lacking an alternative, we supplicate Him or Her or It to help us out of our misery.

We live in perpetual conflict with our ego-consciousness, which feels our isolation, and with a consciousness liberated from the rational mind, which perceives the unified connectedness of all things. Thus, in the presence of an illusory I, only the belief in a singular, human-like God can win the upper hand.

Despite all this, prayer helps. Whether we know it or not, when we pray, we speak to our own essence and not, as we have thus far believed, to a separate entity.

If the Divine is truly segregated from us, how do our prayers reach those or that prayed for? When we pray, we speak to ourselves. Or, in other words, the One being speaks to itself, which is why it hears prayers and responds in its own way.

If you receive Divine help, you receive self-help. This is incomprehensible to the ego, which is why so many people still believe God is an independent, omnipotent being.

For centuries, we have been led to believe that we are dependent on help and judgment from above. Branded into the collective subconscious, this delusional thinking demotes most of humanity to impotent beggars, barring us from the truth – the Divine is not what we think it is. The Divine is much closer than we believe it to be. Now, let us discover together just where the Divine is.

Where is God?

What and where is God? The following questions will help you find out. Take your time with this exercise. Absorb each question, answer it and then move on to the next one.

If there is an omnipotent God, is He all-embracing and omnipresent?

Does God embrace and penetrate you, too? Each tree, flower and atom?

If God embraces you, are you then also in God?

If God penetrates you, is God then in you?

If you are in God and God is in you, are you then also an aspect of God, also Divine?

If you are also Divine, is there a difference between you and God?

If God encompasses and penetrates all things, then are all things God?

Is »your God« still alone, isolated from you and all things, »up there« in heaven?

God is everything and expressed through all things. God is every human being, every dust mote, every breath of wind and every thought. God is Life in the present tense. God does not exist separately from you. He-She-It is not somewhere else. God is also you.

The king said to his wise man, »I will give half of my kingdom, if you can show me where God is.« The wise man replied to the king, »I will give your kingdom twice over, if you can show me where God is not.«

Although you understand the truth of these words in the core of your being, you may still fear God's wrath. Will you have to do penance if you fail to follow God's will? Have you already failed in the eyes of God?

When your body perishes, what we usually call »death«, you will not find yourself standing before an ultimate judge who will then decide your doom. Over the centuries, millions upon millions of people have believed a religious institutional lie, despite the fear and anxiety it generates. Or rather, *because* of the fear and anxiety it generates. Fear constricts, fear oppresses.

The ego is terrified of Love. The ego is terrified of the Divine because authentic, unconditional love dissolves the ego. Where all-embracing love reigns, there is no place for a horror-stricken ego. Because the majority of humanity identifies with their illusory I, they fear Love. Although, love is often praised as the highest and most desirable achievement, this love usually refers to a personal bond with another person or thing.

Living with a perpetual feeling of isolation, the ego's greatest fear is the fear of death, which is compounded by the terror of being judged after death by a humanoid, stern God (a projection the ego created itself).

Since the ego rejects everything that it cannot claim as its own creation, it also rejects the Divine. From the perspective of isolation, the ego creates a super-power, invincible opponent. For the ego, reconciliation is not an option. The only remaining possibilities are attack or expulsion.

Since the ego has no concept of veritable Love, knowing only damnation and judgment, it assumes that sooner or later it will be punished for its rebellious behavior against God. This delusion intensifies the fear in a person identifying with his or her ego many times over.

We desperately long for love, but fear love will punish us. Yet, the belief that Love or God would punish us is just one of the ego's major creeds, and perfectly illustrates its insane, contradictive character.

A contradictive character that has bred to the age-old, colossal fallacy regarding God's essential being, wreaking countless wars and collective powerlessness on humanity for millennia. Still, you can liberate yourself here and now. The only one

judging you is yourself. Absorb this insight into your consciousness and throw open the doors imprisoning old beliefs.
Release yourself to the freedom of Life here and now.

You may ask yourself if it still makes sense to use the word
God, laden as it is with damage done and done to it. If you
are no longer comfortable addressing God, you can replace
it with something more neutral, such as Life, Being or
Consciousness.

Keep in mind, though, that any name is nothing but
a fleeting idea, emerging from the rational content of your
awareness, which is steeped in the necessary duality for our
everyday, »outward« lives. There, where our consciousness is
quiet, devoid of »I am«, there is no concept of God.

Regardless of the stillness or motion flowing through your
consciousness, you remain untouched by rational concepts,
living in unity with the divine source.

Probing and Insight

Since your childhood, you have been convinced you are an »I« with a name and a history, suffering pain and doomed to die. Despite what you think, this is not your Life. If that statement gives rise to uneasiness or denial, the following thought experiment may lighten the load.

The questions to come may sound rather dramatic, but imagine that modern medicine could keep you alive no matter what. Now, answer the questions as spontaneously as possible.

A body

Do you believe you exist?

If you do, do have a sense of self? Do you feel alive?

Would this feeling of being alive vanish if both of your legs were amputated?

Would you still feel alive if they cut off both of your arms, too?

Would you still feel alive without your upper body?

And what happens to your sense of self when you have no eyes, ears or thoughts? Is it still there?

Where is this sense of self? Is it embedded somewhere specific in your body?

Does your true being have anything to do with your body at all?

As you just realized, the profound sense of self is neither diminished nor erased when there is less body to house it. Ergo, you are not your body.

Since the beginning of time, humanity has been misled by the belief we are an organic being of flesh and blood. Although this is not true, it is certainly not an invitation to view our bodies as annoying extra baggage, something to ignore, reject or neglect in the name of »spiritual progress.«

Our bodies are valuable, sensitive instruments and without them we would not be able to perceive and recognize our essential being. How would we experience our aliveness; how would we read these words without our bodies?

You might now ask yourself, »What am I then, when not my body?« You will soon realize; the seeker is the sought.

Mortal fear

A survey in the U.S.A. revealed that many people fear speaking in public more than they fear death.

From the ego's point of view, speaking in public could trigger a worst-case situation. Our thoughts and images, our »me« identity, would then be exposed and open to attack. We identify with whatever we are presenting, and any opposition from our audience endangers the presentation's (our) very existence. Should the presentation be challenged, the ego is equally endangered. We do not consciously call this »mortal fear«, instead we call it »stage fright.«

Our own, physical death seems less threatening than public exposure. Perhaps because dying is an abstract idea, lying somewhere in the indefinite future. We cannot see death approaching, so it seems less threatening at the moment. And anyway, for our ego, death is a relief, liberating us from life's eternal struggle.

But when we speak in public, we enter a premeditated, terrifying situation. When things go badly, we feel attacked, demeaned, found wanting. Insecure and dissatisfied, the experience lives on inside us long after the speech is over.

We often find ourselves subconsciously battling for our survival. We are edgy and afraid. If we are at odds with someone, we are afraid. If we want to stand up for ourselves, we are afraid. Our egos' mortal fear has countless shapes and infinite levels of intensity.

Compounding this is our identification with an illusory »I«, that binds us closely to our body and the knowledge of its mortality. This dependency on our body magnifies our terror of death enormously.

Another thought we lug around with us is, »I have only this one life, so I have to make it count for something.« Driven by the need to achieve, we chase rainbow after rainbow, looking for the pot of gold. We want to reach a goal, formulated by our fantasy and promising ultimate happiness.

Knowing we are going to die, we strive for ever-higher, never-before-attained achievements in art, sports, economy or science.

The flip side of the successful future coin is our fear of death. On the one side, we hope the future will be better, on the other we know that death is lurking everywhere. Hope, fear and anxiety huddle closely entwined.

To flee the dilemma of mortality, we dream of a future that remembers our name, our existence. Perhaps in a piece of music, in a work of art or in our children. The coming generation should hold a piece of us; we should live on in the future.

All this effort is not only useless, it is superfluous. There already is an effective antidote to death. There is no need or possibility to create one. The antidote is the awareness of your present, living essence, that what you truly are. Let us go further down this path together.

Death and emotions

Say you receive a call that a loved one has died. The natural, spontaneous reaction is grief. You hear the news, hang up the phone and cry.

This is a healthy and appropriate reaction to losing someone you love. You surrender to your grief, you brave the feeling. This is part of coping, of adjusting to new situation without suffering any sustainable damage. You are not suffering, you are grieving. There is an essential difference. You may feel a powerful, inner pain, but when you allow it to be; when you feel it, it will pass through you and fade away.

Once more you hear of a death, but this time, in addition to your grief, a thought construct arises. You think, »What will the poor man do? He's lost without her. Surely, he'll die soon, too.«

As if the situation isn't sad enough, the ego has to top it off with a fantasy, turning pain and grief into suffering. Now, we are trapped in imaginings that make crocodile tears of our natural weeping. The ego is secretly pleased, having created a drama and a suffering so essential to its survival. In such situations, the ego often appears on the outside to be the saddest, most pitiable creature or the most compassionate human being on Earth.

Learn to differentiate between emotions and feelings. Emotions are simultaneous, bodily reactions to the ego's thought processes, lending credibility to its judgments of a given situation. A self-righteous ego, for example, would argue, »The very thought of it makes me sick to my stomach, so my version of the truth must be right.«

Feelings such as rage, grief or joy are often valuable indicators of why Life is the way it is at a given moment. Put more trust in these as in your thoughts.

But when you mistake emotions for feelings, you become entangled in complex imaginings of your rational mind and cannot recognize them as the lies they are. This makes life much more exhausting. A pure feeling feels true, no matter which feeling it may be. You can take it in and feel it completely. Don't worry, it's not going to kill you.

An emotion, on the other hand, often feels simulated, like a drama put on for your ego's entertainment. Sometimes, when emotions arise, a part of our body reacts by contracting. The thought patterns in your head suddenly intensify in number.

Be attentive and wary of this refined, inner tumult and distance yourself from it, giving it little importance. Stories and emotions come and go, come and go.

Here is an easy equation to keep in mind:
Pain is not suffering.
Pain + Thought inventions = Suffering

Lie down and feel

Do you have repressed feelings you shy away from? In the following healing exercise, you will experience that your feelings will not destroy you. Quite the contrary, they will show you the way to freedom. This exercise takes a bit more time.

For the next hour, turn off all possible disturbances such as the telephone or doorbell. Lay down in a comfortable place, where you feel secure. Maybe on your sofa, on a mat on the floor or on your bed. It is important that you feel sheltered and will not be disturbed.

When you are lying comfortably, close your eyes and breathe gently and deeply in and out through your nose, letting your belly rise and fall. If you cannot do this, then simply breathe through your mouth, keeping it relaxed and slightly opened. Focus attentively on the gentle rise and fall of our belly. Don't worry whether you are breathing correctly or not. Your breath will take care of itself. Everything you are doing is good the way it is. Be tranquil.

Now, either in your mind or out loud, say, »Every feeling inside of me may be here now.« With this statement, you create an inner approach to what's inside you. You allow everything to emerge without judgment or condemnation. If you have an issue with fear, speak to your fear. Say to your fear, in words that feel right to you, »Dear fear, you may come to me now.« Stay serene and keep breathing slowly and gently. The fear of what will happen when your fear emerges is usually greater than the feeling itself. You will survive anything that wants to be witnessed by you.

Be loving to the emerging feelings. Greet them as you would your own children. Face the feelings, feel them entirely, embodying an attitude of love and acceptance. The feelings will come and go. They have accompanied you throughout your life, until this very moment. Nothing could ever have been otherwise, and even repressed feeling serve a purpose that we don't always comprehend. It is enough to feel them and thank them.

It is important to let the feelings occur, not to understand why they exist. Analyzing them would twist the intimate moment into a delusionary thought-invention, hindering the integrating process.

For example, when a feeling of fear arises, stay attentive. Don't think. Feel.

Perhaps you feel a cold or prickling sensation rising from your feet and spreading throughout your body. Be open, approach the sensation thusly, »Aha, so that's what my fear feels like. Hello fear, it is good that you are here now.«

Accept your feelings, tears, emerging thoughts, your body's reactions and observe all of these things impartially, with playful interest and curiosity. Stay tranquil, internally serene and simply keep breathing.

After a while, the fear may fade away and something new emerges, maybe grief or rage. Remain open, observing and welcoming the new feeling as you did the one before. These feelings will also pass through you, eventually giving way to something you may not have reckoned with – joy.

The ego cannot explain this mood swing, which is understandable, as the ego has always been the sealant on your store of life's joy, without ever knowing it.

All feelings are right and may exist right now. They are neither good nor bad. They do not want to kill you, they want to belong to you, be seen and felt. Beneath all so-called negative feelings such as fear, rage and grief, lies the joy of Life. Joy arises when you penetrate layer after layer of thought and emotion, becoming aware of your true nature. Joy of Life is a deeply satisfying, highly spirited feeling. Joy makes evident what you are – the one Life, come home again.

When you sense you are finished with the exercise, breathe a few times in and out consciously, slowly and deeply. Open your eyes and go quietly and confidently about your day.

I absolutely must…

Remember the apple exercise? This time, you will be using a sentence containing the words, »I must.«

Close our eyes and repeat three times, *I absolutely must reach/become/achieve…* filling in the blank with something very important to you.

Observe how your body reacts much more intensely; how the thoughts and reactions appear much more urgent than they did with the neutral apple exercise. The word »I« brings about this more powerful emotional reaction, as we normally wholly identify ourselves with this word.

As mentioned before, we hold thoughts containing the words »I« »me« »mine« and »my« as the absolute truth. Yet, even in this case, the »I-thought« arises spontaneously and you are the silent witness that can observe it. The content, the thought's statement, still has nothing to do with your true nature, and it never will have.

You may ask yourself how is it possible to follow a thought exercise without producing the thought? This may seem like a paradox, but you will soon see how it works. It may be helpful to imagine you have »ordered« this thought, not personally created it.

You are not the arising thought, you are the observing consciousness, witnessing the thought as it emerges. The same thing applies to emerging emotions.

Thoughts and corresponding emotions emerge simultaneously. In the earlier section, *The Pendulum*, is an example of how your stomach clenches when you think of a certain person at whom you are terribly angry. It's not an »I« that is angry. You are the one observing the entire ego-anger reaction – thoughts and their corresponding emotions – without judgment, and untouched by them.

This insight is liberating as it also frees you from the belief that you *have to* achieve something in your Life. Each and every compulsion is caused by magnetic thoughts, drawing your attention and talking you into doing things. They have nothing to do with your true being, so you needn't act on them.

This is why I recommended earlier that you strike the words »should« and »have to« from your vocabulary, permanently.

Words off the page

Most of humanity believes the rational mind is an independent unit, like a computer, creating and controlling processes. We believe these processes include thoughts, inner images and perhaps even emotions and feelings.

Apparently, we own a bustling system that perpetually compiles, processes and acts on information in a myriad of ways.

This is an enormous fallacy. The rational mind understands nothing, absorbs nothing and cannot act or react in any way, shape or form. It is nothing but tides of thought, coming in and going out, created and witnessed by consciousness.

But we believe our rational mind can actually, actively do something, can actually understand things. Yet the »understanding« that we ascribe to our rational mind is a misleading word. Our rational mind is nothing more than our thoughts themselves. We have misunderstood.

We believe our thoughts are created *within* our rational mind, giving this mysterious system an identity and authority that it cannot possibly exercise because it doesn't exist.

We usually read our thoughts like lines written in a book entitled *Rational Mind*. This is a good analogy, except the book they are written in does not exist. Thoughts do not arise *inside* the rational mind, they *are* the rational mind. The lines – our thoughts – exist. The book – our rational mind - does not. A thought, a line of letters, can neither understand something nor do anything. It is simply an apparition created by Life. Consciousness perceives the emerging content. Or to put it more simply, perception takes place. There is nothing you can do about it.

So, say goodbye to the illusion of a rational mind that can understand, act or create. Countless thoughts appear, a jumble of letters, that at some point was dubbed »rational mind.« Jumbles of letters cannot understand anything, nor can they absorb anything or produce anything. They appear and disappear.

It is important to grasp these words in their entirety. Every one of us fears losing our mind. The idea makes us restless. Losing our minds means losing control means going crazy. Fortunately, the opposite is true. You can't lose your mind because your mind does not exist.

Perhaps, soon, there will be fewer thoughts inside you. Perhaps, soon, it will be utterly still. We could then say you truly have lost your mind. And you will enjoy it, without a trace of fear. Naturally, some thoughts will reappear, and you may sometimes wish you could just as quickly lose your mind again.

As self-probing will soon reveal, there is no one who thinks. Thoughts arise out of stillness. Therefore, you cannot influence them. There is nothing particularly brilliant about a rational mind you can neither control nor stop. So, there's no need to try and be especially clever or intelligent. Such efforts are ego-machinations, striving for security. Be willing to simply *be*. Any intelligence you may need will come without your input.

Life is the source of your river of thought. Life determines content, quantity and quality. When you think which thoughts is completely out of your hands. Much content seems to refer to a personal »I«, creating corresponding bodily and emotional reactions.

Know this – the »me« and your rational mind are one and the same thing, they are thoughts. To believe the thought »I think« is to differentiate between an active »I« and the passive thought process.

By personifying I-related thoughts and their corresponding emotions, we fall prey to the delusion of controlled, personal action. This generates an illusory I, the ego. This is nothing but grand theater. Now, you can see it for what it is.

Who thought that?

When you do this exercise, be detached. Forget for a moment everything you have heard or learned about the brain, thoughts and consciousness.

When you begin the exercise, perceive what happens. That sounds very easy, but our thought processes have become so complicated, that we no longer recognize simplicity.

»To perceive« means to accept what is, as it is, without giving credence to the added mental scenery that hypnotically distracts us from the here and now. There is nothing wrong with our thoughts as they crop up, but we can perceive much more than mere thoughts.

The point is to balance the scales; to create a healthy equilibrium. Swept away on a flood of thoughts, we distance ourselves even further from Life's abundance. Everything is an ingredient of Life; the quality is in the blend.

And now the exercise.

Sit down comfortably for a while in a place where you will not be disturbed. Sit quietly. Assume an attentive, watchful position, like a cat patiently and watchfully waiting at a mouse hole. Observe your thoughts as they come and go, without commenting on them. Fully embody the silent witness.

Close your eyes and ask yourself silently, »Where do my thoughts come from?« Bide your time. Maybe other thoughts arise. This is not the true answer to your question. Ask yourself now, »Where do these thoughts come from?« Bide your time. See what happens.

You may experience a moment of thought-less silence. This living stillness is the true answer to our question. All thoughts are born of this stillness. No matter how hard you look for a thinker inside of you, you won't find one. There is no cogitator, no I, producing thoughts. Thoughts arise, period. There is no »me« making them, »me« in itself is just a thought. You are only a thought.

Life, Being or Consciousness creates the thoughts appearing in this body – that which we have always believed to be »me.« Thoughts are generated and emerge from stillness, for no reason we can fathom. You are not only flesh, bones and thoughts. You are the stillness that creates, perceives and witnesses. You are the silent consciousness, encompassing all its manifestations.

Deeds without a doer

This profound insight, that there is no thinker, grows into the awareness that there is also no person thinking. »I think« is nothing but a thought, without identity, and incapable of creating thoughts independently. A row of letters can neither produce more letters nor do anything else at all.

Since there is no person doing anything, there is no perpetrator. Which is not a license to kill, saying, »I didn't do it, I don't exist.« Behind all occurrences there is no *individual* action manifesting them.

Things happen, and then other things happen, which we call consequences (or cause and effect). In conscious awareness, devoid personal actions and/or personal responsibility, running amok would be the most unlikely result. Our physical organism retains its basic conditioning and tendencies, further determining our actions.

If you have no murderous tendencies, you will not kill. Besides, the non-existence of a personal I does not mean the rest of the world will condone your violence. If one organism shoots another, the perpetrator will probably end up in jail.

It's all a game, following certain rules. In Buddhist and Hindu philosophy, it is also called »Maya«, the great illusion. You may not exist, but by doing something, it happens.

No one is right when it comes to classifying actions as good or bad. Everything that is, is.

The world surges between apparent opposites like electricity flowing from plus pole to minus pole. A bad guy is followed by a good guy, and vice versa. Creation expresses itself in countless variations, balancing everything out without judgment. There is no one here and no one there *personally* doing anything. Liberate yourself from the burden of past entanglements, from those people you have rejected for whatever reason. Thus, the fallacy that »someone else« has intentionally done something to you dissolves.

Liberating yourself from guilt liberates your fellow humans from guilt, directly bringing about forgiveness.

»Well then«, some may say, »if there is no one here, why bother to do anything? I could just as well hang out on my sofa, doing nothing.« Sure, you could. But you probably wouldn't, if you are prone to activity. We are lively and creative beings with the drive to express our aliveness; to do things. All the same, you can be lazy or active, however you like.

Conscious response

Do what you will, and it will be done. Say »yes« to this moment and act on it, when necessary.

Saying yes to here and now, confirms and accepts a given situation. This can just as well mean, clearly saying »no« to current outer circumstances. Thus, develop an attitude of »Okay. This is the way things are. What do I want to do with it?«

If you are in a situation that is uncomfortable for you, and you are in a position to change it, stay composed, saying, »No, I don't want that.« This stance allows you to remain active without battling the present moment. If you greet the present moment with, »This shouldn't be this way«, you make things hard for yourself. You oppose what already *is*, upsetting the balance within you.

You may think there is a trivial difference between the inner »yes« and the inner »no« attitudes, yet it has an enormous impact on a life in balance. »Yes, things happen. How do I handle them?« This is acceptance; a conscious attitude toward Life.

A product of the past

I once received a letter with the following question, »When I am not the product of my past experiences, what am I then?«

Looking with an open heart, you will realize that there is only the given moment. Everything referring to the so-called past is nothing but images and thoughts arising in the present tense.

If you were to show me a photograph and say, »That's me a couple of years ago«, I would ask you, »When does this photo and its story arise?« After a moment's thought you would say, »Now.« And that's correct.

Along the same lines, there is no future, it is only a thought construction emerging in the here and now. If I were to call you up from this moment onwards, again and again until the following day, each time asking you, »What time is it now?« you would answer again and again, »It is now.«

So, you see, there is only the present tense and we cannot escape it. This revelation throws open the doors, inviting you to redefine yourself, letting go of the so-called past. The past is nothing but a mental image with a powerful story. Emerging in the here and now, it draws us in like a magnet, captivating our attention, creating a thick fog between us and conscious, empowered Life right now.

Do not attach so much importance to your past – it does not exist. Most people cannot see this because their ego needs the past to identify with and to function as a scapegoat.

So many people cannot live their true-Life expression, although they have long become adults and live in the present tense. They are still holding their parents and other people responsible for their current suffering. When there is no other person to take the blame, something the ego rarely allows, they blame their earlier self for missing chances or making fatal mistakes in the past.

You are not the product of your past. You are the expression of this moment – your present feelings, thoughts and actions. The moment you cease to believe your thoughts on the alleged past, you are free.

But don't take my word for it. View these words critically, as it is much more exciting and fulfilling to probe into yourself; to gain your own insights; to discover what it is thinking these words that bind you to the past.

You will discover that there is no one there. There is no thinking person. Thoughts come from nothing; from living stillness. Everything takes place in the present moment, including those thoughts referring to an apparent past.

Realize that past and future cannot exist without the light of the here and now, but the here and now exists without the past or future. Thus, the present is the *only* reality.

Imagine this unity as an energy matrix, perpetually configuring and reconfiguring the present moment. Literally *everything* occurs simultaneously, so-called experiences, memories, feelings, convictions, stories, and so on, without cause and without effect.

You did nothing, neglected to do nothing, suffered nothing and learned nothing in the past. This may be difficult to see right now, yet you bring nothing with you from the past, as you are only timeless present.

Life

Look around for an object that belongs to you. A glass, for example. Now, think the thought, »I have my glass.« What would happen to your person, to your I, if the glass fell down and shattered?

»Nothing«, you would most likely reply, »would happen to my person. A shattered glass has no impact on me.«

This is true, of course, due to the subject-object relationship between you and the glass. There is no apparent connection, and the loss of the object (the glass) has no negative impact on the subject (»me«).

We often think, »I have only one life.« If you believe in reincarnation, then you would think, »I have only this life.« What would happen to your person, your I, if this life were to fall and shatter?

»I would be dead« or »I would die«, would be your most likely reply.

Now, that is odd, because the thought referring to your life is basically no different from the thought referring to the broken glass. Although both are cases of I-object relationships, the consequences of an ended life are far more dramatic than those of a broken glass.

In the first case, the »I« is untouched by the shattered glass. In the second case, the »I« is destroyed. How can that be? Assuming you owned a life, as you owned a glass, then nothing would happen when this life is shattered. But of course, this is not so. Again, you may ask, how can that be?

The thought, »I have a life«, is simply wrong. It is a delusion. Life is not an object. Life encompasses all things. What appears to be a paradox loses all discrepancy when we understand this:

You do not have a life, you *are* Life.

You cannot exist beyond Life as you can beyond the lifespan of a glass, a house or a table. Therefore, it goes to follow that you do not have Life. You can only *be* Life. The thought that we have a Life is a fallacy; an illusion.

For many years we have suffered under the belief that we are only this body and this rational mind. »When this organism falls apart, everything is over.« This concept may sound very familiar to you, but it has nothing to do with your true nature.

Life is living. Life is neither death nor dying. Life neither decays nor passes away. Life lives and continues to live for eternity, that is Life's core attribute and its essence. It cannot be turned inside out, it has no opposite. Your existence means you are a part of Life, indistinguishable from Life itself. This is an amazing revelation with colossal impact:

You are Life and you are immortal.

This revelation may surprise you and you find it hard to immediately accept. Don't worry about it.

Feel what this thought triggers inside of you, »I am Life and I am immortal.« Do you feel joy? Life, you, reads these words, recognizes itself and is delighted. Allow these words to sink in. Eventually the whole picture will become clearer. As soon as you absorb and accept your immortal essence, things will change in ways you have yet to imagine.

Instant Karma – Paid in full

The concept of reincarnation in Buddhist philosophy inspires moral and compassionate behavior. The idea of karmically correct comportment in order to overcome an earthly existence, is a valuable guideline for many people.

Perhaps you have already heard of Karma and reincarnation, or believe in it yourself. Karma is a kind of »account« of things you have done in this or a previous life, which have an impact on this or coming lives. As long as your Karma is not paid off or is not balanced, you are indebted to the circle of life and must be reincarnated.

Your faith tells you that if you cannot pay off your debt in this life, i.e. attain enlightenment, it would be best to be reborn as a human being, at the top of the evolutionary ladder. However, if you do manage to attain enlightenment, you will be liberated from the vicious circle of earthly suffering and no longer need to be reincarnated.

There is one essential error in the idea of reincarnation. Namely, that there is no past and no future, only the present moment. You cannot be here from a former life. Besides, here is no individual I. So, who can be reborn? Who can become enlightened? And when could anyone do this in which non-existent future?

Images and experiences under hypnosis, past life re-visitations or consciousness journeys all take place in the present, and only in the present. All the same, they are understood to be indications of a time-axis.

Consciousness experiences itself in billions of ways simultaneously and is connected to everything. Some people may delve into an exceptional version of here and now, thus believing they have lived at another time, in another place.

But we were never a king, a beggar or anyone else in another life. A consciousness liberated from the personal I knows that only this moment, and this moment alone, occurs. Consciousness *is* this moment.

Recognize the eternal present moment and the illusion of an individual existence. You need never again hope for future salvation. Be attentive and aware in this moment and all Karma is instantly swept away.

»Since there is no self, there cannot be any after life of a self, but there are deeds and the continued effect of deeds. There are deeds being done, but there is no doer. There is no entity here that migrates, no self is transferred from one place to another; but there is a voice uttered here and the echo of it comes back.«
(Siddhartha Gautama, »Buddha«)

Of free will

Sit down in silence and probe into the decisions you have made today. How many of these choices occurred independent of other events?

You will probably discover that not one of your decisions was unrelated to other events, since each and every decision was made in relation to other, emerging mental images. You exist within an interwoven mesh of events, and every decision you believe you have made independently, is actually a reaction to Life's impulses already formed within you.

This network of impulses is a key component of the timeless present and you are an inalienable aspect of the weaving.

Although there is no free will, you feel as though you are doing what you want to do. This is fine and dandy, but you cannot detach yourself from Life's will. Everything exists and occurs in the present, including contradictory thoughts that propound the opposite.

When you hear this for this first time, sensing the truth behind the words, you may ask, »Am I nothing but a divine marionette?« For a moment, you may feel more powerless than ever.

Yet, everything occurs without an »I« muddying clear waters. You are lived by Life. Or, in other words, Life lives itself.

When you grasp the profound truth of these words and accept them fully, any sense of threat or limitation gives way to a joyful sense of freedom and deep tranquility.

Relax, there is no one there who can do anything. But should you »play the part« in this »theater«, things do occur, and you have countless options to choose from.

The void of I

Touch a piece of clothing you are wearing with your finger-tip. What do you feel?

You'll probably say, »The cloth, of course, what else?« Right. But how can you feel the cloth, when your fingertip is a real, solid substance? Wouldn't you feel this substance instead of the cloth? Or feel both the cloth and the substance of your fingertip? But you don't. Why?

The explanation is as simple as it is amazing - The essence of your fingertip is a void.

And just as your fingertip is a void, so is the illusory, personal I. Perception can only take place because the essence of this I is a void; is nothingness. All perception, including thoughts and feelings, are directly absorbed by your true being. An »I« can never apply them; can never stem the flow.

There is no middleman, no »me« between consciousness, you, and perceived content. It is only perceived content and does not require anything personal to interpret it. Yes, thoughts arise, insisting they are a person, an »I«, but this is not true. So, let them pass by and observe them as superfluous commentary.

This small exercise focuses on exposing the illusory character of your chimerical I, the ego.

To describe this phenomenon, I sometimes use the word »void.« You will find the term »void« or »nothingness« in many spiritual works, albeit, it is rarely explained. It may be that these words trigger discomfort, as we imagine a dark and subconscious abyss, from which there is no escape. This is compounded by our ego's anxiety, as the words depict the ego's own lack of substance.

However, the void or nothingness is not your true nature. Your true nature is a living, vibrant stillness. Your true nature is Life's abundance, creating and perceiving all things.

You are not the void from which emerging content arises. You are the void and the void's content at the same time. Without the slightest boundary or division. This is what is meant by »Everything is One.«

Perhaps you can already sense the unity. As perception occurs, the »I« is a void. Your true being contains all manifestations, it is the abundance of Life.

Fragmented reality

As you observe a flower, the observation of a flower occurs. What use is the addition, mental commentary, such as, »Is it a tulip or a rose?« The flower is there and living, whether tulip or rose does not make it more real or more alive.

Quite the contrary, once named, the observed object loses vitality and freshness.

Be attentive, and observe how often everything you see, hear and feel is automatically smothered in thoughts. Life remains just as vivacious without this running commentary. Turn toward the stillness and let the world be as it is.

When you are inwardly still, the universe reveals to you all its beauty, right now. You may suddenly become aware of the birdsong outside. They did not just start singing, the have been singing all day, without you taking notice. Nearly every ounce of your attention has been turned inward toward your thoughts, emotions and feelings.

Look around you and observe your thoughts each time your eyes come to rest on an object. Are you immediately bombarded with the object's name? With stories connected to the object? With emotions and memories related to the object?

This process is the automatic allocation of everything you see. The ability to allocate objects and circumstances is indispensable for practical purposes. Without it, our communication would be arduous, to say the least. Still, at the same time, naming and filing away each and every object each time we see it, only serves to shatter unified reality into a million tiny fragments.

Life and its manifestations are perpetually changing. It is impossible for our so-called rational minds to absorb or grasp this multifarious fluctuation. Yet, this is what it ceaselessly attempts to do. And the result is usually a sense of being hopelessly overwhelmed. »I don't get it. It's too much for me. I simply don't understand.«

The exact opposite of what we are trying to achieve, occurs. Thinking will never satiate our hunger for understanding, for control, for security and for connectedness. We cannot succeed because the ego's own contrariness is destined to fail.

Control does not lead to security. Control leads to fear because control, by definition, includes doubt. The need for control is essentially the fear that something could go wrong. Striving to find peace of mind, we often think, »I just need to work harder, then I will find peace.«

This thought drives us in the wrong direction. Already anxious, additional mental efforts to alleviate anxious circumstances only drive us further from unity.

Probe into this mental scenario. Expose its fallacy, and it will dissolve. Your true self can then re-emerge and you are safe, connected and at home.

The flying submarine

You are sitting in an infinitesimally tiny, flying submarine. You launch into space and view the world with new eyes. Atoms, electrons and neutrons appear like colossal mountains of energy or tidal waves.

How do you know where you are? Are you in space, in a table, in a human body or in the wall of a house? The dimensions have changed and what you saw, in your human form, as individual, distinct objects, is now one single tapestry of energy.

Thoughts appear like bolts of lightning on the horizon and vanish again. You are so much smaller than they are and watch them flashing. The world is new and unfamiliar. Is it possible, in this universal unity, that a separate, singular I can exist?

From this vantage point, you realize that all things are connected; that segregation does not exist. A consciousness identifying with one body, however, has no other choice than to view everything from the profoundly limited perspective of humanness. But this fragmented, distorted perception is not reality.

Opinions and judgments about what is going on in the world are wholly dependent on your perspective; on your point of view. Take a moment, and put yourself in the place of another living creature. Be a bat, a dog or a fly for a while.

Which perception is right? You will quickly understand that there are endless, equally valid realities and our perception cannot possibly be the end all be all of existence.

From a scientific point of view, matter is made up of atoms, molecules and energy components that we cannot even grasp. What we call matter is ninety-nine percent space.

Our human conviction that the world is made of solid, individual and separate objects, corresponding to how we see it, has absolutely nothing to do with reality. Thus, becoming aware of unity is not a process, taking place within a body. Unity encompasses all of the so-called outer world as well.

Know this: there is no inward, there is no outward.
You are *everything* that perceives and is perceived.

The unidentified object

Take a glass and place it in front of you, on a table. If you don't have a glass at hand, use something else. Observe the constellation before you and describe it in your thoughts. »The glass (or whatever) is on the table.«

Now, imagine you have never seen a glass or table before. You haven't the slightest idea what they mean, how and of what materials they are made, or what purpose they serve. You also have no concept of distance, intermediate space relationships or atoms. You sit before this unidentified object as an extra-terrestrial, seeing this thing for the first time.

How would you know that the glass and table are *not* a single unit? The glass component certainly looks differently than the wooden component, but this may simply be the structure and nature of the apparition. Without your mass of compiled mental concepts, you would not immediately assume that the glass and table are two separate entities.

Look around you now and let go of all categorical concepts. Imagine that all things emerge simultaneously. Feel your innermost reaction as you observe your surroundings, without thought commentary. Be quiet, be tranquil. How does that feel?

Is it more peaceful? What do you feel when you merge your entire being, your inner and outer self, with this unified vision?

»You«, with all of your thoughts and feelings, also emerge simultaneously within the Unity of all things. Without your thoughts categorizing and fragmenting, you perceive all Life as Unity. Nothing you perceive can harm you. Everything belongs to everything, as it always has. You simply forgot.

Remember now. All things are One.

Why not?

Everything this moment brings forth appears in the web of consciousness.

When you take pause and perceive your thoughts, you realize that they arise spontaneously, without any effort on your part. It is all part of cosmic theater in which an illusory »I« also plays a role.

Allocating and identifying shatters emerging Unity into millions of individual units that cannot be grasped in their diversity. We are often overwhelmed by the sheer mass of input. Humanity is not meant to *break down* and *understand* each individual aspect of unified creation. Humanity is meant to *feel* and *experience* the wonder of unified creation in its *entirety*.

Yet, our curiosity drives us to constantly try and understand cosmic theater. And we just as constantly fail.

Why things happen is the great mystery. The question, »why?« has no answer, as everything is as it is. Even the person asking the question is an illusion. Should something be other than it is, it would be other.

Thus, distance yourself from thoughts demanding, »Things should be different than how they are.« We are probably the only creatures housing thoughts and images that deviate from the present occurrence.

Accept the fact that your inner images and thoughts are rarely aligned with here and now. Accept what goes on inside of you and what you find directly in front of you.

Do not think of a feast when all you have is dry bread. And do not wish you were somewhere else, unless you can go there right now.

Change your situation when you feel this is the right thing to do and it is within your power to do so. Do not try to bend or suppress the current moment by surfing the waves of contradictory thought. This will only cause you stress and suffering.

Simply take joy in what is blossoming in front of you. Whether it is a flower, a shrub or a weed plays no part in how or how deeply you enjoy this manifestation of Life. And who really cares what its Latin name may be? Observing the world with analytical eyes destroys unified beauty. But maybe your botanical education gives you the sense of being better than others.

You believe you know so very much, but you see nothing. You miss out on the joy waiting to suffuse you in moments of »thoughtlessness.« Know nothing and see everything.

Look around this world and realize how unnecessary and strenuous it is to question why this or that, why »beautiful« and »ugly« exist. Everything is here in an equilibrium we cannot fathom. Your answer now to the question why is, »Why not?«

The sun is rising,
a bird in flight is singing.
The dewed leaves shimmer golden.

Life is a miracle.

The Freedom of Being

Life makes everything available all at once - actions, thoughts, feelings and other perceptions. This coherency works like a brilliant play, captivating us again and again.

At first, we have no idea where the story will lead us. It's like we are standing on stage, unaware that we are in the middle of a play. We take the roles Life has given us very seriously.

Every now and then, someone gets wise to the kind of play being enacted here. These wise people are then called »enlightened«, »awakened« or »liberated.« But, despite their unclouded vision, these people, too, are bound to the theater and cannot simply abandon their places on stage. As opposed to other cast members, they can and do no longer take their roles so seriously. They continue playing, with more ease and levity, acting *as if* everything is the way it seems.

So, whether you have been given the role of a king, a beggar or victim, you can now see it is all a play. Roles, dramas and stories come and go. Everything changes and everything is as it is.

For a large part of your life, you have been a seeker. Perhaps your quest has been for the pinnacle of spirituality, for unity, or for God. At the least, you have been striving to feel at home in Life. Now that you have come so far, you know that there is nothing »out there« or »up there« that will quench your longing and end your quest.

You already are the one Life, a divine expression. The sought is the seeker. Consciousness has been playing hide-and-seek with itself and wants to find itself again.

Life and the longed-for paradise take place right now, and only right now. Be glad you no longer need to chase rainbows. The beauty of existence lies at your feet. Misleading thoughts have made the past years incredibly difficult. Yet, everything is so easy because you don't have to do anything. Just be here and take care of things as well as you can.

Choose to live Life easily.

I am

Think back on the exercise »should and have to.« Using your own name this time, close your eyes and think three times, »I am *name, surname*.« Observe how your body reacts to these thoughts.

This probably seems truer and more familiar than the thought from the »should and have to« exercise. Consciously repeating these thoughts and sensing their impact, you will see that your body reacts differently than it did by the previous exercise.

The reason is easy to pinpoint. Your name was the first thought-form your bodily organism absorbed after your birth. From earliest childhood on, your true self has wholly identified itself with this body and this name.

It may well be that this is standard procedure in human life, all the same it represents the greatest distraction from the truth. You are not »*name, surname*« no matter how strongly you believe it or how powerfully your body responds to it. The name and its history are only roles in the cosmic theater, performing – alongside other content – on the stage of consciousness identifying with this body.

You remain nameless, immaterial consciousness, untouched and untouchable, perceiving this body and its given name.

Soap bubbles

Our human body has a variety of sense-organs through which perception takes place. We no longer pay all too much attention to these perceptions as we have accustomed ourselves to them since birth.

We consider the sensual impacts coming from the outer world to be personally irrelevant.

On the other hand, we consider our thoughts and corresponding emotions, our natural feelings and our bodily reactions to outer stimuli as personally relevant events. The combination of these varying inner apparitions is the sum of our identification, our »me.« We consider our bodies and the bustling activity it contains to be our true selves.

We believe our compiled experiences empower us to correctly categorize, assess and judge the world – both its external guises and our internal machinations. Yet we know nothing of the true source which births all these phenomena.

Should someone ask, »Who are you, really?« We only shrug our shoulders. Or, if an answer is proposed, it probably goes something like this, »I am the sum of all this. This body, my rational mind and perhaps my soul, too«, indicating the body.

But how can an »I« judge the world truthfully when it does not even know itself? Our own Life foundation is clear as mud, so how can we build truly stable structures, offering steadfastness and sanctuary? Deep down inside, our ego knows it has no veritable substance, which is why it feels permanently threatened by its environment. Nonetheless, this peculiar mechanism is hell bent on survival.

The soap bubble refuses to burst.

Under normal »me« circumstances we focus primarily on our inner commotion. Being out of balance, we experience a sense of gloom since many of our thoughts and emotions are discomfiting.

In quiet equilibrium, we are attentive to and perceive inner and outer occurrences equally. In other words, when we are in balance, we can be conscious of the simultaneous emergence of all things. In balance, our thoughts play a much smaller role, thus allowing a great many more pleasurable things in Life to penetrate our consciousness. This new, healthful blend brings more clarity and vitality to our lives.

Believing that »I« perceives all occurrences is a delusion of mammoth proportions. In truth, all content is perceived equally *without us*, we just don't notice it.

We are not »me.« We are *pure, transpiring consciousness*. Pure consciousness is aware of all emerging content, all internal bustle and all external occurrences. The »me« we believe ourselves to be is made up of thoughts, images and feelings – a mere fragment of all emerging content.

It goes to follow then, that a sense of self is superfluous to conscious perception.

All things prevail without the »me.« All content, all Life, carries on without this facet of the consciousness spectrum. Nothing is lost, nothing is missing.

The soap bubble bursts.

Good night, ego

As you know, perception changes when we sleep. The content of the »real« world becomes the content of the dream world. Consciousness is prevalent as we dream, otherwise dreams would not be dreamed. Moreover, we usually feel we are personally experiencing the surreal dream adventures.

The ego, ever out for control, also occasionally aspires to take control of our dreams. With steady training, it is possible to realize you are dreaming as you dream and to redirect the plot of your dreams. This is called »lucid dreaming«, and denies the sleeper true recuperation, which is the whole point of sleeping.

While sleeping, consciousness aims to relax, taking time out from the dream of the »I.« That lucid dreaming is psychologically and physically beneficial is dubious, as it only serves to cement the ego's powerful hold, instead of dissolving our identification with it.

Some spiritual traditions use lucid dreaming as a tool to help disciples recognize the dream state of the waking world, preparing them for their own death. It is believed that a variety of phenomena and events occur in the *Bardo*, the in-between dimension, after the body dies. Lucid dreaming training aims toward enabling practitioners to remain conscious after death, where they then have a choice between optimal reincarnation or entering pure light, liberated from the circle of Life and reincarnation.

This is yet another story the ego tells, striving to maintain control until the very end. The ego's compulsion to control all things in life arises from its omnipresent terror of death. The ego craves security and believes it is only safety-net provider. The world would stop turning if the ego is not there to keep the ball rolling.

As we move from our nightly dream phase to deep sleep, consciousness is still active, but »I« is dormant. Do you have panic attacks or feel threatened during deep sleep phases? Can you be oppressed or annoyed?

As opposed to the dream phase, nothing perceivable occurs during the deep sleep phase. The ego, your rational mind is dead. An identifying you or I are no longer participating, there are no ego-stories to tell.

Although the ego believes Life cannot go on without it, Life *does* go on. The body breathes, the heart throbs, metabolism and blood flow are uninterrupted. Nature's processes take care of themselves, oblivious to irrelevant machinations of the rational mind.

And though Life enjoys experiencing itself through your body, or better, *its* body, you will eventually wake up again. Fresh as a daisy and well-rested, you are closer to your true, essential nature than you may think. You are literally fresh as a daisy, as your consciousness recreates itself anew every moment.

Life, you, lives on. Whether thoughts, images, dream sequences, sense of self or nothing occurs is wholly irrelevant. So, relax, and don't take yourself so seriously.

Among friends

You are sitting with friends or relatives when you are suddenly struck by the banality or aggressiveness of their conversation. So much blah blah. There are moments you can hardly stand it and your basic impulse is to just get up and go. But not wanting to make waves, you stay put and bear it out, feeling increasingly isolated where you had once felt quite at home.

Not so long ago, you would have joined the discussion with enthusiasm, but now it leaves you cold, and your mutual interest has mutated into isolated annoyance. Some of your friends have become strangers and you do not understand what has happened. It seems the more conscious you become, the less tolerant you are.

Do not let this development unsettle you. It is a step in the growth process. When looking at the world and your life with new eyes, you suddenly become aware of things you hadn't noticed before. You were once a part of the unconscious majority, but consciousness is awakening from the dream world of thought and is striving to find itself again.

For a while, you may feel like a traveler between two worlds. Your true self is eager to expose all fallacies, striving powerfully toward consciousness. On the other hand, consciousness is still partially under the dominion of rational thought and is afraid to let go of its old existence. You may feel torn, wondering if this new consciousness is really worth the effort and price to be paid.

But you will soon notice a transformation, as once uncomfortable situations no longer upset you. They are simply no longer significant.

Not that you are indifferent or insensitive. Quite the contrary, you with feel profound compassion and love for your fellow humans still controlled by their egos. The arrogance and rejection you felt during your growth period will dissolve of itself.

There is no one here. There is no one there. Everything is an expression of the one consciousness and you can serenely observe the play from a conscious perspective.

Should you hear a statement coming from your milieu that no longer applies to you, then let it go, it's nothing personal. There is no one personal present who could say anything you disagree with.

Discomfiting situations occur to increase your consciousness and fall by the wayside once they have fully fulfilled their purpose. Furthermore, your subconscious, pre-conditioned need for conflict, relying on reactions from your surroundings also becomes a thing of the 'past.' Your teacher, Professor Suffering, may retire from the lecture hall. And you are free to do the same.

Remind yourself of the ego's penchant for judgment and condemnation. Now you know why judgments are senseless. You see but a fragment of the whole picture. But even more importantly, there is no one there to pass judgment or to pass judgment on.

So, let judgments pass, then no one can denounce you and you cannot denounce anyone. No one person exists. You are the One consciousness, eternally free and secure.

Super heroes

As you awaken to your true being of pure consciousness, you may fall prey to a new illusion. Imagining that consciousness is everywhere leads some spiritual seekers to believe (and hope) that, once liberated, they can appear anywhere in the universe just by turning their will to it. They aspire to so-called consciousness journeys or to out-of-body experiences.

This complicates matters. The narcissistic desire to attain super powers via spiritual liberation is spawned by no other than the »me« seekers believe they are overcoming.

You may have read trustworthy accounts of »enlightened masters« who have left their bodies, only to appear somewhere else, or have been seen in two places at one time. These stories have nothing to do with awakening.

On the contrary, they are food for a hungry ego, striving to be better than or go beyond us mere mortals. It is crazy to think, »As soon as I am enlightened, I will have super powers. I will never need to sully myself with the ordinary, everyday world again.«

In the Theater of Life, consciousness animates this body at this time on this planet in order to perceive itself. The consciousness or perception that we are is bound to this physical form. During this human existence, we cannot travel to other worlds for longer periods of time. In deep meditation, we may experience unity with the true source. Yes, this is otherworldly and for a while we may be cradled in its silence, beyond thought; beyond our bodies.

But eventually we will be called back to our physical form, simply, perhaps, because we desperately need to use the toilet.

Here, again, we can call up the image of a stage. We can acknowledge that we are actors in this Life, playing a temporary role. This helps us to remember not to take everything so seriously. And when the play is over and we leave the stage, our true nature once more has the opportunity to recognize itself.

Liberating ourselves from thought or ego-identification is about attaining serenity, ease and inner peace. Once we cease identifying with the »I«, we experience an all-encompassing connectedness. You no longer feel alone in this world, you are awakened, recognizing that you are everything and nothing.

The revelation that you are the entire universe also means that you cannot detach yourself from it. You are not Superman flying through the galaxy to the rescue. There is no individuality. All perception of all things is you, belongs to you like one, big family. You have come home.

No one here at all

When we have fully grasped that no individual person exists, we may at first feel utterly alone. There is no individual partner, no parents, not even a house pet. You may think, »Here I am, abandoned and stranded in the universe.«

In philosophy, this attitude is called *solipsism*, defining the doctrine that nothing exists beyond one's own consciousness of self. Well, you cannot possibly be alone as there is no »you« and there is no »me.« It is not *your* consciousness that perceives, perception simply happens. You have not expanded into a giant »me«, replacing the mini-me of your ego with a spiritually developed grand poohbah, master of the One consciousness. There is no »me« in any form whatsoever.

This feeling of isolation is a remnant of persistent identification with the illusory I. When you recognize the illusion of this final shred of »I« and let go of the thought structure, you will realize that Being is all there is. Being as a verb! Being as an active occurrence, not a static state of existence. Perhaps we need to invent an innovative word for this, a verb that describes perpetual motion like »beinging.« In the effort to grasp the ungraspable, we use the noun being, while »beinging« eludes us.

We are caught up in thought, trying to understand, categorize, define. Being cannot be understood, it can only be experienced. You are not being or consciousness. The state of being *is*. The observer permeates the observed, and vanishes. All that there is, is what is. That is all.

This is a revelation. In its essence, it deviates from all other statements uttered thus far. The step by step progress, the repetition and steady evolution of all statements thus far were necessary detours on the road to awakening.

This roundabout route dances around stumbling blocks and fallen trees thrown in the path by a consciousness hypnotized by a thought-obsessed »I.«

We are approaching the one, true source of all Being. Suitable words are becoming more and more difficult to find, as words are born of duality.

Words are not truths. Words, at best, can only sketch out and try to reflect the One. Words cannot reach the One, cannot replace the experiencing and awakening to the One. Read these lines with your heart and allow your true nature to see itself.

No one perceives. Perception happens.

Death follows dying follows death

Death is the opposite of birth, not the opposite of Life. Life continues. Life has no opposite. All the same, the human body eventually deteriorates. We call this Death. What then?

Although we cannot really know, there are several possibilities. It may be that consciousness attaches itself to a physical form without inner thought processes, such as a small, single-celled living being. In this case, we would not be plagued with ego issues.

Another variation is that consciousness identifies with a life form including thoughts, as the human organism does. Here, an organism can once more take part in the Theater of Life, considering itself an individual, separate me. With a little luck, this human, too, will rediscover his or her inherent consciousness.

No matter which version of Life after death we believe in, nothing awaits *us* because none of the options encompasses *individual*, momentary attributes, feelings or yearnings.

It may help to know that no separate consciousness exists that can be transferred onto another life form. Only the *One* consciousness exists and may choose to identify once more with an allegedly separate manifestation, for a while.

Without an individual I, there is also no sense of time. Hence, after the body dies, no one exists. No one has to wait someplace nice or someplace nasty for the next step in events, such as rebirth.

Since Life has no opposite, your true self cannot die. Maybe it takes on a new shape, maybe it doesn't. The human body passes away, as all things in the manifest world pass away. Know that passing away and immortality are the two immutable truths applying to all living creatures. You may find peace in this lifetime.

Friend or enemy, all are the same. This insight brings you connectedness, brings more light in the world and contributes to a more aware collectivity among the human family.

In quietude

Although there is no one there who can achieve something through exercise, there is a possibility to experience how it is without an »I« for a while.

Be tranquil over the next few minutes, do not try to achieve anything. Remember, everything is done and you can do nothing, as you do not exist. And yet, should you »do« something, it happens.

Sit down comfortably somewhere you will be undisturbed. Observe your thoughts as they come and go. Close your eyes, if it's comfortable to you. If not, leave them open. While observing your thoughts, they decrease in volume. Try to remain still and be attentive to possible gaps between your thoughts. The gaps may become larger and the stillness shining through them grows proportionally inside you. Feel this stillness, see if you can feel it throughout your entire body.

Possibly, thought will stop entirely and all that remains is living presence. Should that be, abide in this feeling, linger in the presence as long as you feel comfortable.

Should you be able to feel the stillness inside you, you have had a momentous experience – you can exist without a mental construct called ego. When the illusory me vanishes, or is reduced, your body does not fall down dead. Quite the contrary, Life, you, experiences itself much more profoundly in a body without thoughts.

Thoughts will return and that is fine. The point is to establish a healthy balance between moments of thought and moments of inner stillness.

I recommend doing this exercise every now and then. Allow your true nature to emerge and stabilize in an intention-less, ego-less condition.

The illusion of enlightenment

»Enlightenment« or »awakening« is the ultimate destination of spiritual seekers and must be attained at all costs. But who is seeking enlightenment?

This time, the ego cloaks itself in holiness to achieve a stronger position. A »me« sets out to become enlightened. But since there is no »me«, the efforts are nothing but vanity.

It is impossible for a person to be enlightened or spiritually awakened. What could be further awakened in Life or being? Thoughts? The body? Consciousness? Life is already awakened, it couldn't be more awake. Yet, consciousness *can* liberate itself from its identification with an illusory person, and the thoughts and emotions that shape it.

You could call this event consciousness »awakening« from the dream of »I.« Yet, even if the I illusion remained permanently installed, it, too, still occurs in perfectly wakeful consciousness. You cannot leave the present moment and its inherent wakefulness.

You cannot attain a separate, »higher« condition beyond this world, then the I bearing these hopes is only a dream image made up of thoughts and emotions.

When you detach yourself from your identity, something no one can achieve or influence, you merge into lightness, joy and connectedness with the world. You may not have super powers or constantly experience extraordinary perceptions, but your Life will be more serene. The colors of the world seem more brilliant and you perceive sounds that were muffled by obsessions with thought. The ordinary becomes the extraordinary; becomes that which you have always sought.

Feeling and perceiving Unity is sought, which is simultaneously the seeker. Being experiences itself as being, in every way, shape and form. It makes no difference if it realizes this or not.

Often, the quest for living presence hinders us from being just that. Our thoughts and feelings are so busy with seeking, with assessing our spiritual development, we fail to see the spirit of being right in front of our noses. The search hinders the finding.

Individual enlightenment and personal awakening are fantasies, emerging as equally valuable scenarios in the theater of consciousness. When these fantasies pass away, you are liberated from the ego's noblest aspiration – to become an enlightened singularity. Now, you have more freedom, serenity and joy. You'll be laughing up our sleeve at yourself and your earnest questing, once you recognize it as Being having fun.

Enlightenment is an awakening to the reality that no one is there to attain enlightenment. Hence, individual enlightenment is an illusion, to strive for enlightenment is inane. With a bit of luck, the one Life will awaken to itself. Yet, no I can influence or accelerate this awakening.

Life without me

After spending so many years chasing after an illusion, it's time to sit back and relax. Have a cup of tea or coffee. Go for a walk over the fields or in the forest, and take pleasure in the beauty around you. The wonderful and diverse world of manifestations is there for you to take part in and enjoy.

There is no limit to what you can do, including further spiritual training, meditation or contemplation. Keep in mind that everything is but a play, there is no personal I who can successfully carry out these exercises. You can do nothing; you can attain nothing, so you are free to do as you will. On the playground of Life, you have many possibilities.

Another advantage to exposing the illusory »I« is that you are free of pride, guilt, envy or hate. Everything occurs without the burden of morality. You are not your thoughts, your worries or your imaginings. You are consciousness, perceiving everything, including itself. This is true for all humanity and all beings emerging within existence. You once took Life too seriously, but now, your load is much lighter.

Observing your inner bustle will sometimes cause you to spontaneously burst out laughing at the nonsensical thoughts that appear. Yet, eventually, the mental carousel slows down, leaving you with your healthy common sense, an equally valid emergence among all others. It is there when you need it, happily bereft of compulsory thinking and an obstreperous, tyrannical ego.

You may become somewhat forgetful as unimportant things aren't worth holding on to and simply dissolve. Don't worry yourself about it, it's part of the process. Come to Life playfully and much will come to you with wondrous ease.

The twelve steps from I to Being

The following twelve steps offer you orientation on your path to awakening. It begins with the illusion of being an individual person, defined through time, experience and genetic makeup.

Each step takes you deeper into dissolving the illusion of a personal I. However, it is highly unlikely that your evolution will proceed in the organized fashion depicted here. Profound awakenings can occur spontaneously, all at once or in an arbitrary order and sequence. No two paths are alike. All things occur, as they occur.

I am singular and do as I will.
I have a personal age, name and this body. My past, the sum of my experiences and talents, as well as my genetic makeup define who and what I am.

I am not my body.
The sense of existing continues, even when my body is diminished. Hence, I am not my body.

I am not my thoughts.
Since I can observe my thoughts, I am not my thoughts. I am the perceiver of these thoughts.

I am a singular consciousness.
I am neither body nor thoughts. Hence, I am a singular consciousness perceiving body and thoughts.

I have no will.
Thoughts, feeling and physical reactions emerge without my input. Hence, I have no will of my own.

I am an expression of Life's will.
As I have no will and am completely propelled by Life, this physical organism can be taken as an expression of Life's will.

I do not exist and there's nothing I can do.
Since I am neither body, thoughts nor will, I do not exist. Thus, there is no individual I that can willfully change this. Without individuality, there is no individual consciousness.

I am nothing.
I am not an individual person. I am not an individual consciousness. Hence, I am nothing.

I am everything.
Perception and content occur. Without perception, there is no content; without content, no perception. Perception and content are equals. Hence, I am everything.

I am.
To believe I am everything, is another mental concept. Since I am not mental concepts, I let them all go. I do not know what I am. I am.

I am not.
There is no I; not in any form or shape. So, there is no »I am.« Hence, I am not.

Being.
Being happens now.

Out of the dream

That's all there is. There is no past. There is no future. As time does not traverse, there is neither cause nor effect. You have neither cause nor effect. Hence, you do not exist.

Without cause and effect, nothing is fixed in time. Everything is timeless. Nothing has taken place, as there is no time separating or chronicling events.

You are here, where you have always been. You repose in the source, you have never left. Everything is an expression of the one loving source. Nothing has ever left here.

Life dreams. Life dreams it is its dreaming. And when Life awakens, it knows itself as the dreamer, and is joyful.

Epilogue

Thank you for reading this book. I sincerely hope it has helped pave your way to free being, allowing the light of consciousness to shine brightly within you. Perceive your true nature and gift the world with your expression of it – this is your destiny.

When you next open this book, you may have the feeling that its content has changed. It hasn't. You have. Thus, you can discover ever-expanding profundity, in these words and in yourself. You are increasingly present.

Perhaps you will recommend this book to a friend, as its sole function is to bring more consciousness to this world. Perhaps you desire to find someone who will guide you along the way. It can be a great inspiration to encounter a here and now human being in the flesh, furthering your journey to unity, freedom and inner peace.

The greatest teacher, however, is what you have always been, Life in this moment; unconditional love, free and at home.

Terminology

Awakening: a conscious disentanglement from personal identification. Consciousness exposes the fallacy of being a singular, human being.

Being: as a verb. Fluid awareness and perception. What *is*, right now.

Consciousness: the emergence and perception of all phenomena, including perception itself. Comparable with »I am.«

Ego: the illusionary I, a mature construct invoked by emerging thoughts and emotions with which the consciousness identifies.

Emotions: bodily reactions accompanied by emerging thoughts. Not to be mistaken for spontaneous feelings.

Enlightenment: highest goal of a spiritual seeker. Usually associated with attaining profound personal perceptions, abilities and permanent bliss.

I: a thought arising in consciousness. I am only a thought.

Identification: when consciousness adheres to emerging thoughts and the corresponding emotions absolutely. Thoughts and emotions produce the sense of me.

Illusion: the image of being a singular, personal being with a singular, independent fate. Also see Theater.

Liberation: when consciousness releases identification with thought (the rational mind) and the sense of a personal I which accompanies thought. Acknowledgment of equality in all occurrences.

Rational mind: all emerging thoughts. Thoughts do not appear in the rational mind like words in a book. Thoughts *are* the rational mind. The words, the thoughts exist. A rational mind without thoughts (a blank book) does not exist.

Theater: also called Maya. Illusion, the obscuring power, veiling the real and depicting the unreal. The Life plays hide-and-seek with itself, the grand or cosmic theater.

Exercise index

Acknowledgments

My deepest thanks go to Sofia Karassawas who supported this book wholeheartedly from the outset. I am grateful to all the people who have accompanied me thus far. A very warm, heartfelt thank you goes to Ramey, without whose wonderful, sensitive, unerring and competent translation this book would have never seen the light of the English-speaking world. I am profoundly grateful for my family and for all friends and fellow human beings I have had the honor to meet. You are all the light of the world.

Thank you, Life, for your joy in being this moment.

About the author

Dirk Hessel is a spiritual teacher and an international author who was born in Germany. He was manager of an international company and author of a TV series. While searching for a deeper level of existence, a profound transformation of consciousness radically dissolved the identification with the I. Dirk Hessel has written several spiritual books. Without ideological restrictions, he gives lectures, readings and talks on conscious existence and deliverance from the illusory I.

Dirk's work has already inspired many people throughout Europe to find inner strength and a fulfilled existence. The central core of his teachings is to permanently see through the identification with the I and to fully accept the present moment. Once this has happens, the path to inner peace opens and thus can contribute to peace for whole mankind.

www.dirkhessel.com